'YOUR FATHER AND I NEVER MARRIED'

Uncovering the secrets of my family

Rick Lovering

ISBN: 979-8-4413-5650-3

Dedicated to members of my family that are no longer with us- my parents, my brothers Simon, Bob and David and my step-mother, Claire.

CONTENTS

ACKNOWLEDGMENTS

My thanks to the following:

To members of my family who helped me by telling me stories about my parents and other family events. My brother, Colin, and my son, Tom, for offering advice during the editing process. My nephew, Tim, for his research into the genealogy of my family and analysis of the DNA results. My son, Michael for helping me with my father's military records. Contributors on Ancestry UK and My Heritage genealogy websites. Also, members of The Lovering Group on Facebook, Major Kevin Pooley of The Salvation Army and Chris Spinks.

To my wife, Pauline, for her patience, support and encouragement throughout the years of research and exploration into the writing of this book.

1   MUM

"You know that Mum and Dad were never married?".

It was not something I expected to hear as we were strolling through the streets of Hereford on a night out in November 1982. It was my older brother, Simon, that had asked the question and I didn't know how to respond to it.

"Eh?", I said, not quite believing what I had heard.

"Mum told me that she and Dad had never actually got married", Simon explained, "I had gone to see Mum about getting my birth certificate sorted out and she said, 'Your father and I never married' and then broke down in tears".

 Simon wanted to apply for his first ever passport as he planned to visit New York with his girlfriend of the time, Vanessa, so he needed all the necessary documentation. My Dad, Lieutenant Colonel Arthur Walter Lovering, had been in the Army so had been stationed at various places around the world such as Germany, Yorkshire and

Cyprus. Simon had been born in Rheindahlen in Germany which made getting a birth certificate a little more complicated. That was why he had gone to see Mum to get further details. There had been a problem with the date of the marriage between Mum and Dad. For a moment, I still did not know what to say as various thoughts went through my head. I tried to make sense of the bombshell statement. Mum had always told us that she was Marie Cremin, an Irish girl born in Macroom in Cork, who had married Dad and had six children. They had separated when I was quite young, so I never really knew my Dad. It now turns out that I never really knew my Mum either! If they were not married, then that means all six of us were born out of wedlock. Now, as a secondary school mathematics teacher, I expect some of my pupils would like to call me a 'right bastard' on occasions when they felt I was not being fair towards them. Now, if it ever happened, I would not be able to argue with them as I am a bastard! Other questions were raised. What happened to the real Marie Cremin? Who was Mum?

When we got home, we made some tea and coffee and discussed what we knew about Mum and Dad. As it turned out, very little as far as details were concerned. We did not even know the year when Dad married Marie Cremin, but our eldest brother David had been born in May 1948, so we assumed it was before then. Dad had been in the Royal Artillery during the Second World War and I vaguely remembered someone saying that he was involved in Italy and had been at the attack on the monastery at Monte Cassino. The last time I remember seeing Dad is when he visited us in Eastnor in

Herefordshire when I was about 6 or 7 years old. He had been working for the Ministry of Defence in London. The last address we had for him was in Middlesex. Rather bizarrely, I also remembered seeing a picture of him with some well-known actress opening a Wimpy Bar in Nottingham. Quite how he became a manager of a Wimpy whilst in the Army or working for the M.O.D, I did not know. Maybe it was some sort of undercover operation and if so, I hope he didn't wear a Big Mac as part of his disguise! He re-married later and went to live in Malta where he died in 1982. David, plus brother Christopher (Bob), born September1949, and sister Peta, born November 1951, were much older than us so might know a bit more about him. We wondered if any of them knew the true situation regarding Mum.

Given that David was born after the War, we surmised that maybe Dad and the real Marie Cremin had drifted apart whilst he was away fighting the war. He had probably met Mum sometime after he had returned home. That was something that I imagine was very common as partners could be separated from each other for possibly years and the experiences, both being left at home and fighting on the battlefront, would undoubtedly change people in many ways. We then asked why did Mum assume Marie Cremin's identity? I had a copy of my own birth certificate which clearly stated that my mother's name was 'Marie Lovering, formerly Cremin' so it was clear that officially Mum was Marie Cremin. We reached the conclusion that maybe Marie Cremin had refused to divorce Dad or that he had lost complete contact with her and was unable to get a divorce so Mum pretended to be her instead. As Dad was in the Army, it might have been awkward for a married man to have a mistress so, as no-one had actually met Marie, then everyone would assume that Mum was really her.

I had spent pretty much all my life living with Mum, apart from two years living with my sister and her family and being away at university in York for four years. I should, therefore, had known a lot more about my Mum's past and I tried to recall any stories or snippets of information I may have heard from her. How many of those stories were true? It could be an issue given she had lied about her identity all these years. She had told us that she had grown up in North London and that her father was a keen Arsenal fan. Ted Drake was a real hero for Mum too and she supported Arsenal. She told us that she used to know a gateman at Highbury Stadium who would let her into the ground for free, just so she was able to see Ted Drake play. Arsenal were certainly a successful team in the 1930s. Apparently Dad was a Tottenham fan so maybe Spurs winning the double in 1961 was the final nail in their relationship! She also recalled going for walks around Regent's Park and visiting the zoo. Certainly, her accent suggested London connections, so I had no reason to suspect this was not true.

Mum also used to say how her life was tough when she attended a Roman Catholic Convent school in Louvain in Belgium. Quite how she ended up there, we never questioned. I was beginning to realise that maybe we should have enquired more at the time when she was reminiscing. We then may have found out why she was in

Belgium. The Catholic part would obviously fit in with her roots being in Ireland so it may have been part of Marie Cremin's life instead! She described in some detail how the stone floors were freezing when she had been set some punishment by the Mother Superior for some misdemeanour. It was hard to imagine she was making it up.

Mum had also visited other parts of the world in her life as well as Belgium. She once told me all about the Maori people and their customs when she had been staying by Lake Taupo on North Island. For a girl from North London in the 1930s, New Zealand was quite an exotic place to end up unless her parents' work had taken her there. Maybe her father was a diplomat or something similar. That would explain why she had been placed in the convent whilst they were away on business and that, occasionally she travelled with them, for example, to the other side of the world. That might also explain how she somehow attended one of the Nuremburg rallies! It might be that my memory was playing tricks on me and that she had only visited the site of the Nuremburg rallies since the family did have two separate stints living in Germany. The first was when Simon was born in 1955 and then, after a short spell at Strensall, near York when I was born in 1957, we returned to Germany and my youngest brother Colin was born in 1959. We obviously thought she attended the actual Rally as we often referred to her as Eva Braun, partly because her knowledge of Germany and the culture was so good. In light of the recent revelation that she was not Marie Cremin, maybe she was Eva!

Mum seemed to cram a lot into her early years as she also claimed to have attended Royal Holloway College, or it may have been Bedford College, in London. Quite an achievement for a woman in the 1930s or 40s when many fewer women went on to Higher Education that do nowadays. I don't recall what she studied but I think she said it was something like History. She would have been attending university around the time of the Second World War depending on how old she was and that reminded me of another conundrum. We didn't really know her date of birth!

Mum celebrated her birthday on 12th May – it would be interesting to know the date of Marie Cremin's birthday – and Mum said that she was born in 1926. She told us on another occasion that she had actually forgotten her true year of birth as she had lied about her age in order to join the Forces during the War. Even if it were true that she had to falsify her age on application forms, it is quite staggering that she really forgot her true year of birth. Of course, it might be that was because she was getting muddled with her personal details and those of Marie Cremin as part of the lie. Having joined the women's branch of the Royal Air Force, Mum told us she worked at Fighter Command and was one of the women that moved the airplane identification blocks around the table map in the operations room. Whenever there was a war film on television, we would watch eagerly for a scene where a squadron might be in trouble or the Luftwaffe were approaching. They'd show the position on the map with little marked blocks. "Hey Mum, is that you there?", we'd ask. Mum used to tell us about how a place would be set at the dining table for all the pilots and there would be empty seats at the places where a pilot had not returned from a sortie. She never really said much about what she did during the war though she once told us that she did not enjoy hearing the carol *Silent Night* as it reminded her of hearing the German prisoners of war singing it.

Talking of her age, another fact that stuck with me was that she said she was ten years older than Dad. Being a naïve youngster, I took that to mean that every husband was ten years older than his wife. When I reached the age of ten, I thought 'my wife is now only just being born'. That belief obviously turned out to be false as Pauline, my wife, is only two years younger than me. False also because Dad was not Mum's husband!

Another time when I should have had my suspicions about Mum was when I went to the Varsity rugby match between Oxford and Cambridge Universities in 1970. It was a trip organised by my school, Ledbury Grammar School in Herefordshire, and I was thrilled to be going to the world-famous Twickenham stadium. In those days, we were quite poor so rarely went on holiday or even day trips so travelling to London was a big deal for me. At the match, I bought some team rosettes and the matchday programme. The programme had a list of all the students that had represented Oxford or Cambridge in the rugby varsity match. These people are known as Blues. When I got home, I showed Mum the programme and she noticed the list of Blues winners. She took great interest in it and told me her father had been a Cambridge Blue. It was only later that I had a look at the list and could not find anyone called Cremin. I thought this odd as Mum had studied the list quite closely but I did not think to query it with her at the time. Now I was beginning to wish I had, if only to hear her explanation for his omission.

Our Godparents might also give us some more clues about Mum's identity. Auntie Joan and Uncle Eric were Simon's Godparents. I think they lived in Fulham so I might be able to look up their address. Perhaps they were really our Aunt and Uncle by birth rather than because they were Godparents. My Godparents, Willie and Sinie Schutte lived in South Africa. How did Mum and Dad get to know them? There were also the Lenhams who visited us in Ledbury with their daughters Jane and Susan. I don't think Bob and Barbara Lenham were anyone's Godparents so what was the link with the family? Just old friends of Mum's or maybe relatives?

We had no photos or documents from the past including, even, pictures of us when we were younger. This was because in the 1970s they had been put in a biscuit tin and were in the possession of Bob when he was living in Hereford. The tin was put in a crate which was left behind by Bob when he moved to a new home. It would be so good to see some pictures of Mum and Dad from the 1940s and 50s or, at least, just a picture of them together.

There was also the story that Mum had another child before any of us was born. Her name was Carol but she had died either at childbirth or, at least, a very early age. Mum was told that she would not be able to have any more children. She managed to have six more though she did say that after Peta (her third – or fourth if you include

Carol), that Mum and Dad decided to have no more children. There was a four-year gap but another three children followed, including me. In many ways, we three youngest were probably the closest of the siblings, mainly due to our upbringing. There was also the family joke that youngest brother, Colin, was not actually one of the family because they had brought the wrong baby home from hospital!

There was another major reason we should have asked Mum regarding her being Marie Cremin and that was that all her friends knew her as Helen! I guess we thought that might just be a nickname or possibly her middle name which she preferred to use. My older brother Bob, after all, was really called Christopher John Lovering. The name Bob stuck with him, as toddler brother, David, could not say the word 'baby' and said Bobby instead. My sister's middle name is Helen or Helene which might suggest that that was indeed Mum's real name, rather than Marie.

By the way, Simon got his passport sorted and was able to travel to New York. Later in the year he visited Israel and Egypt as well. He had certainly got the travel bug which was to last a lifetime and see him visit over one hundred countries. He had a map of the World and he would colour in a country once he had visited it. Getting that passport had another consequence though as we sought to find out the truth about Mum. Who was she and what happened to Marie Cremin?

2 DAD

Although the revelation that Mum and Dad were not married had a big impact on us, it was more than four years before I started doing any real research into finding out some facts. I guess we all had busy lives and, since Mum was still alive, there was always the chance that she might one day tells us the full story anyway. None of us wanted to ask her directly, I suppose, because of the fear of really upsetting her again. She probably feared the truth being revealed as she had lived a lie in all official documents, benefits, etc and could end up being prosecuted for fraud.

I decided that I needed to find out some dates of birth and marriages and order certificates, so I could obtain more details. In those pre-internet days of early 1987, it meant going to Catherine House in London where the registers of births, deaths and marriages were kept. It was on a chilly January morning that I caught the National Express coach from Bristol to London Victoria. It was a good journey as a film was shown to keep the travellers entertained. Given that the bus called at Heathrow Airport and, therefore, some of those on board might be flying off somewhere, I thought it was quite amusing that they were showing the film "Airplane!". I hoped that there weren't any nervous fliers on the bus.

Catherine House was a fascinating place as there was shelf after shelf of volumes of records. Between the shelves were slightly sloping tables where researchers could place a volume to search through. There were separate sections for Births, Deaths and Marriages. I headed to the Births section first as I wanted to find out when Dad had been born. Each volume represented a Quarter of a year and the names were arranged alphabetically. I knew Dad's birthday was in August and I figured he was probably born after 1910 so I started from there. I quickly found out that these books were quite heavy, weighing several kilograms, so it was quite hard work lifting them off the shelves and on to the table. The task was made harder if there were many people researching the same shelves as a space on a table may not be by the shelf you were working at. Eventually, I found Dad's entry in the 1913 volume. It was quite exciting to find what you were looking for after lugging several books from the shelves to the table and back again. I looked at the entry for a few moments and thought that might mean Mum was born in 1923 if I went by the 'ten years older' story. I found a form so that I could order a copy of the birth certificate. I would then have to wait for the order to be processed and the certificate sent through the post. Whilst in the Births sections I thought I would look up and order the birth certificate for my sister Peta to check the spelling of Helen or Helene.

Next, I headed to the Marriages section to try to find the record for Arthur Lovering marrying Marie Cremin. I was not sure where to begin so I figured they were married before the War and worked backwards from 1939. It was quite demanding lifting and replacing the volumes once more but so exciting when I found the entry for December 1932. Dad had got married at a rather young age which quite surprised me. Maybe, given Marie came from a Catholic family, they had been forced to get married due to a pregnancy! I had only spent three hours in Catherine House but I was quite exhausted and needed some fresh air. After grabbing something to eat, I was back on the bus heading home, this time being entertained by the film 'Nickelodeon'.

When I got home, I discussed the findings with my wife, Pauline. She pointed out an obvious fact. Dad had married Catholic Marie in 1932 and my brother David was not born until 1948. Surely there was a good chance that they had children in the years before the War. There would be one way to find out – to return to Catherine House and look for births between 1932 and 1948. We might also find the birth certificate for Carol, the baby that died young. So, two days later, I was back on the bus to London, but this time Pauline came with me. It was with a touch of déjà vu that I was able to watch the movie 'Airplane' and look around for people looking a little nervous about flying.

Working with another person made the process of

looking through the volumes much easier. We started with the Births in 1933 and worked our way forwards. We got to 1939 and had still not found anything. It was very disappointing and quite disheartening after doing so much work. We decided to carry on through the War years until we reached David's birth. We kept looking until finally Pauline found an entry for May 1947 which took us completely by surprise. There was an entry for the birth of a Robert Lovering, whose mother's maiden name was Cremin, but he was born in Devon. There is a large Lovering population in Devon so the father could easily have been a different Lovering to Dad. The name Cremin, however, is quite unusual and it seemed too unlikely to be just a coincidence. We ordered the birth certificate but, again, we would have to wait for it to be delivered. Whilst we were there, we looked up some other births to help with the Lovering family history in general. We found the birth of Dad's older brother Sidney and that of his father Leonard Brasier Lovering. Satisfied with a good day's work, we headed to Westminster Abbey to have a look around. Whilst looking at the graves of various monarchs and famous people, I did wonder whether any Loverings were buried there.

Prior to our trips to London, I had visited the Central Library in Bristol to use the telephone directories to look up the address of Eric and Joan Midlane, my brother's godparents. I wrote them a letter asking about how they knew Mum and Dad and whether they had any photographs of them or the family. I was pleased to receive a response from them which included some wonderful pictures of Dad with the three eldest children when they were young. There was also a rare picture of me as a young child with all four older siblings, and a similar picture of Simon as a baby with David, Peta and Bob. As to how they met Mum and Dad, Eric wrote:

"Well it was back in 1945 or 46 when I was working at the War Office in the same department as Arthur. He talked to me of Helen and the baby David and of your Mum expecting her second child. Subsequently I spent a week with her before Bobbie (sic) was born. Afraid I cannot remember the exact location. However, from then the friendship grew and in 1952 your Mum and Dad came along to our wedding".

He went on to say that he had heard from Bob who was asking about the whereabouts of David. He also realised that the date on the back of a photo of David that he had also sent, meant that he had got the dates wrong about the meeting and that it must have been later! Whilst we did not learn any more about Mum's identity from the letter, it did confirm that Mum was known as Helen and the pictures were a delight. I still treasure them to this day. Some years later, Colin was able to visit Joan and Eric at their home in London. When he asked them about Mum and Dad, their reply was 'you'll have to ask your mother about that'. That response could mean a variety of things. It could be that they knew the true story but did not want to divulge the secret. Alternatively, that they had a few sketchy ideas, but Mum would know the detail. Either way, I am sure that they could have given us a lot more information about how our parents got together.

It was quite exciting when the certificates we had

ordered finally arrived. The marriage certificate confirmed that Arthur Walter Lovering married Marie Cremin on 17th December 1932 at the Church of Our Lady of Victories, Kensington in London. Dad was only nineteen years old, two years younger than Marie, and both lived at 9, Gloucester Walk W8. Dad was a hotel waiter and Marie, a waitress, presumably at the same hotel. The wedding was witnessed by Dad's father, Leonard Brasier Lovering, whose occupation was a printer. The other witness was someone called M. Brunton. The certificate stated that Marie's father was a cattle dealer.

Peta's birth certificate confirmed that her full name was Peta Helen Lovering. which provided further evidence, along with Eric's letter, of the correct spelling of Helen. We were now more confident than ever that Mum's real name was Helen, that is until we studied the certificate further. Peta's mother's name was given as 'Marie Hilda Audrey LOVERING formerly CRENIN(sic)'. Hilda Audrey was a complete surprise so maybe Mum's name was really Hilda and she just preferred to be called Helen. This was beginning to get very confusing!

The next birth certificate to arrive was the intriguing one of Robert Andrew Lovering who was born in Torquay, Devon on 28th May 1947. His mother's name was given as Marion Lovering, formerly Cremin. The spaces for name of father and his occupation were left blank, suggesting that Robert was illegitimate. On the right-hand end of the certificate, although not very clear, was the note that Robert was adopted. It would be quite difficult to trace him as he was probably given his adopted family's surname. His mother was not Marie, but Marion. Marion is quite similar and could be a mistake though it still seemed remarkable to find another Lovering, formerly Cremin, and not believe there must be some connection to Marie.

We needed to find out a little more about the Cremin family. I think it was Simon that travelled to Macroom, Cork in Ireland and looked up the birth details of Marie Cremin. He had also found the birth of a Mary Cremin too! Cremin was not an uncommon name in the Macroom area so Mary could be from a different family. When we looked at the certificates he had ordered, we found that both Marie, born 11th December 1910, and Mary Ann, born 5th February 1919, had the same father. He was John Cremin who was a cattle dealer and later a soldier. On Marie's certificate, her mother was given as Hanna Cremin, formerly Hartnett, whilst on Mary's it was Mary Cremin, formerly Hartnett! They both undoubtedly had the same mother but, just as on the certificates of the Lovering children, it would appear you cannot believe everything, even on official documents. The other interesting thing is that the Cremin parents were not very imaginative when it came to naming the children, giving them similar names of Marie and Mary. There was a nine-year gap between them so it was likely there were other children and possibly a daughter Marion who could be Robert's mother though it would be quite incredible if both daughters married a Lovering. Marie's date of birth does confirm that it is she that married Dad in Kensington twenty-one years later. Marie's birthday was 11th

December, but Mum celebrated her birthday on 12th May which confirmed that she did tell us one truth. She was not Marie Cremin, the woman that married our Dad.

The research at Catherine House had given us some very useful information but led to more questions being raised rather than answered. It had also stirred my interest in finding more about my family history and not just solve the Marie/Mum mystery. More visits were made to London over the following year or so. The aim was to find if Dad had any other brothers or sisters who may also have had children. I was keen to find out more about my grandfather, Leonard Brasier Lovering, and his father. Did my ancestors come from London originally or from elsewhere? The surname Lovering is not common but there are many people who share the name in Devon and South Wales in particular. Did my family originate from one of these areas? If so, I was hopeful that it was not Wales as I did not feel the least bit Welsh despite growing up on the Welsh borders in Herefordshire.

We had discovered that Dad had an elder brother, Sidney George William Lovering who was born at the same house as Dad, 2 Balliol Road in London, on 12th March 1911. As on Dad's birth certificate, it confirmed that his father, my grandfather, was manager of a chemist's warehouse. I did wonder what sort of warehouse that might be. It was also strange to think that we had an Uncle Sidney that we knew absolutely nothing about. The only blood relatives I was aware of had been my immediate family; my siblings and their children. I had no knowledge of uncles or aunts and, consequently, of cousins. That is, until now, and it was possible that Sidney may well have children of his own. If we could track them down, perhaps they might have heard stories of their Uncle Arthur and how he ran off with this mysterious woman after the War and abandoned his wife, Marie. A later search revealed that Sidney married Hilda Susie Holmes in 1933 at St Mary's in Barnes in London and that he was a draughtsman. We could not find any records of children being born from then until at the start of the War.

My grandfather, Leonard Brasier Lovering was born on 7th May 1876 in the sub-district of St Peter's in Walworth, Surrey. His father was George Lovering who was a civil engineer and his mother was born Eliza Jones. They lived at 48 Villa Street in Walworth. Leonard had married Catherine Sarah Grindley (my grandmother) on 11th April 1904 at St Mary Church, Newington and at the time he was a Royal Marine living at 185 Brook Street in London. George (my great grandfather) had married Eliza Jones at Trinity Church in St Mary, Newington on 27th May 1860. For at least three generations, my branch of the Lovering family had lived in London which might have explained why I always enjoyed visiting the capital, though I certainly had no wish to live there. At the time I was unable to trace the family back any further, but it had sparked a real interest for me in genealogy. I wanted to visit some of the locations mentioned to feel a part of that history. Whenever I went to London for some event, usually to watch York City play in the capital, I would make a detour to see some locations from the family history. I visited Balliol Road where my father and his brother were born and St Mary Newington, near the

Elephant and Castle, where my grandparents were married. Trinity Church was no longer a place of worship but was used as a rehearsal space for the BBC Symphony Orchestra. I was beginning to feel that I was getting to know my ancestors a little more. I knew what they did and where they lived and got married, having previously known absolutely nothing about them. I had children of my own around this time so would not have so much time for trips to London. Instead I would have to concentrate on nurturing the new leaves of the Lovering family tree. I did, however, make a trip to London to visit Dad's residence in Gloucester Walk when he got married in 1932. The house was nothing out of the ordinary, but it gave me a special feeling to think that Dad and Marie had lived there. It was probably the nearest I was ever going to get to Marie Cremin.

3 DAVID

David, being the eldest of the six children, was probably the one who knew our Dad the best and might also know of Mum's background. The only problem was that we had not heard from him in over thirty years. The last time we heard from him, he was working as a chef in Oxfordshire. He broke contact with the family a year or two after Dad had visited us in Eastnor for the last time. This led us to suggest that maybe David was in fact the son of the real Marie and Dad. When my parents finally split up, he had decided that he had no connection left with Mum!

David Ian Lovering was born on 26th May 1948 in Chertsey, Surrey. As Dad was in the Army and stationed in various places, David attended Ottershaw boarding school. The idea was that his education would not be disrupted by regularly changing schools depending on Dad's postings, but it also meant that he only spent holiday time at home. He, therefore, had less contact with his family.

The family returned from Germany in 1960, flying across the Channel in a Silver City aircraft and, briefly, lived in Hastings. We then settled in Cryalls House in Sittingbourne, Kent. Cryalls House was a rather grand house which was rented out to army personnel families. It was set off the main road of Borden Lane and to reach it you had to travel along a straight drive. The drive was about a hundred metres long with cherry orchards on either side of it. After going through the main gate, there was a circular drive, in front of the house, with a large monkey puzzle tree to the right. Simon, who was about seven years old then, famously thought he saw a ghost in the monkey puzzle tree which caused much amusement in the family. To the rear of the house was a rather large garden filled with a variety of fruit and vegetables including gooseberry and raspberry bushes. One of my earliest memories of my life was standing in the garden watching an aeroplane fly overhead. It is strange what makes an impression when you are just four years old! The house itself was dominated by a splendid staircase that rose up the centre of the house. In the basement was some sort of wine cellar and a scullery with a cold tiled floor, if I remembered correctly. At the top of the stairs were doors to two attic rooms. One of the doors was locked so was always a cause of speculation as to what may be inside it. You could get through a window by the doors and step onto a ledge outside running along the entire front of the house. From the ledge you could peer through a window into the mysterious attic room. We could just about make out some furniture and pictures in

21

the locked room. Perhaps it was filled with treasures! I also remember that we were able to walk along the ledge and drop little stones down the drainpipe. There was an old quarry near the house though it seemed quite a long walk for me. In the quarry was a small hill and it was regarded as a huge achievement when Simon managed to climb to the top of it. He was always the great adventurer of the family who would like to take risks. I don't remember David and Bob being around much- perhaps they were both away at school- but Peta, Simon and I all went to school in Sittingbourne. Simon and I attended the same school. Our journey there, which was quite a distance for two infants, took us past two corner shops where we would buy sweets, if we had any money, which was not very often. On one occasion we tried to buy some penny chews using cardboard toy money and we managed to get to the door before the shopkeeper realised it was not real! My main memory of the school were events that may have traumatised me for life. The school had a main hall which was surrounded by classrooms around the edge of it. One day, when there were medical inspections, I was in a section of the main hall which had been curtained off for privacy. I had been asked to strip down my underpants and suddenly became aware that I was being watched. I turned around to see Simon and some of his classmates staring at me though the glass panels of his classroom that looked on to the main hall. He found it most amusing to see his half naked little brother and was laughing at me with his friends. Another time I was in almost the identical spot in the hall, but this time it was to dance around the maypole. The children had to dance in pairs going over and under the ribbons as we moved round the tree in opposite directions. The only problem was that I did not have a partner which drew lots of comments from the onlooking parents. It was not the last time that I felt I was on my own.

Simon was a cause of much trouble in those days. One day, when we were meant to be in bed, he was messing about with a razor blade. He accidently, or maybe deliberately, cut my finger which began to bleed profusely. Recognising that something needed to be done about it, he sent me downstairs to Mum to have it treated but I was instructed to say that I had caught it in the door! Mum said nothing but I am certain she knew that was a lie. Easter was an exciting time as we had the family Easter egg hunt in the large garden. Rather than just hiding the eggs for us to search for, we were given cryptic clues that led us from one egg to the next. Needless to say, Simon would often cheat or would nick my clues and find the eggs for himself.

I have happy memories of Cryalls House, apart from having to live with Simon; the excitement of hearing a marching band and running down the road to try to see it or going to an orchard to pick cherries for tea. Life was indeed a bowl of cherries but in September 1963 we were to move to another house. It was to be in Eastnor in Herefordshire, on the other side of England. It was going to be a big change for us, but we hoped that it would not have a long drive like Cryalls House. It was probably around this time that Dad was posted to Cyprus and, because the posting was only six months, it was decided that he would not take the family with him. He ended up being there for two years and, by now, the relationship between Mum and Dad had probably broken down. The house we were moving to in Eastnor was part of the estate of Colonel Hervey-Bathurst. Perhaps he was a friend of Dad's through his military connections or it might be that this was another property that was rented out to military folk. Whatever the reason, we piled into a minibus which would take all of us to Herefordshire. That is, all of us except one of the cats who decided he did not want to go and jumped out and ran up a tree just before we left.

For some reason, I don't know what, we stayed in a hotel in Ledbury on our first night in Herefordshire. Ledbury is a small market town near the border of three counties: Herefordshire, Worcestershire and Gloucestershire. It is well-known for its black and white buildings, particularly The Market House, which is a house on stilts in the High Street, and the picturesque Church Lane, which leads to the parish church. The church with a very tall spire is unusual in that the bell tower is detached from the main church building. We were staying in The Feathers Hotel, another renowned half-timbered building which also stood in the High Street and was rather grand.

The following morning, we set off for Eastnor which is about two miles from Ledbury. We got our first glimpse of our new home, The Gables, which was a large detached house at the top of a hill. Next door, halfway up the hill, was a quaint half-timbered thatched cottage which looked very pretty. We then realised that not only did we still have a long drive to the approach to our house from the main road, but that it was now up a hill! Another similarity to Cryalls House, however, was that we would still have a huge playground both within the garden and the surrounding area. Once up the drive, we noticed we had a rather dilapidated garage, with corrugated iron sides and roof, which was by the front gate. I would later get to know that garage quite well when I stepped rather heavily on to the roof and put my foot through it! On passing through the gate, there was a rockery to our left and, as the path bent round to the left by a variety of laurel bushes and other trees. From there we saw the house itself. In front of the house was a grassy bank that sloped down to a large lawn. There was another lawn on the side of the house which led into a spacious garden at the rear with apple trees and other bushes. At the back of the garden there was even an old pigsty. This would indeed be a play paradise for us kids! The house itself had a conservatory built on the front with a cellar, as well, underneath. At the back were some outbuildings which could have been used for a variety of uses and would provide more places for us to play. We were also pleased to see the property was surrounded by a large field on three sides and there was also a wood at the back. The views from the front of the house were quite special too. We could see across the fields, on the other side of the main road, to the southern end of the Malvern Hills, including the distinguished outline of the old iron age fort, Herefordshire Beacon or the British Camp.

Eastnor was going to be a wonderful place to live though we were to struggle financially. It would be significant in that it was the last place where the children of the family would all be together. I only recall Dad visiting us once, but he may have come on other occasions. That one occasion is when we suspect he was saying goodbye to Mum and, possibly, getting her to sign the divorce papers, so he could re-marry. Since Mum was not really Marie Cremin, even if she did sign the divorce papers, technically Dad was still married to the real Marie Cremin. If he were to re-marry, he would become a bigamist! David and Bob had returned from school and spent some time living with us in Eastnor. Peta attended Ledbury County Secondary Modern School, whilst Simon and I went to Eastnor V.C. School in the village. The V.C. stood for 'Voluntary Controlled' and it was a Church of England school. After a year, Colin would attend the school as well. It was to be a tough time for Mum as she struggled to support a family of six children and I don't think we really appreciated it at the time. The hardship she put herself through for her children. She worked some of the time at Malvern Boys' College as a domestic, helping with cleaning and dining duties. The College was about eight miles away and she had to get there by public transport. That meant an early start in the morning and arriving home quite late in the evening. This was the 1960s and, being a woman, I imagine the pay was not particularly great. We were poor, but she still managed to find some money to give us some treats. We would always look forward to her coming home on Fridays because she might bring us some sweets, as it was payday! Because Mum was often out all day, we had to look after ourselves and cook our own meals. I usually ended up doing the actual cooking, Colin would wash up and Simon was chief food taster. Christmas and birthday presents were usually bought from mail order catalogues so that they could be paid for over a period of time. Sometimes the payments were not made which led to even more financial problems. We had a 'book' at the local grocery store where you could buy stuff and pay later. When the bill had risen to a large amount but was not being paid, the shop owners visited the house. We had to hide and keep very quiet so we could pretend we were not at home. Mum always said we would be all right 'when her ship comes in'. After several years we began to realise that her ship had probably sunk and was never coming in after all. I always tell people that we were a poor family, but I think Mum provided us with a rich upbringing.

When David returned home, he had a bedroom on the ground floor at the front of the house. He was always seen as a little different to the rest of us. We thought it very strange that he did not drink tea since it was the staple drink for the rest of us. He preferred to drink squash. David was also a keen fan of The Rolling Stones whereas we were very much fans of The Beatles. I don't think you were supposed to like both groups, even though The Stones' first hit was written by Lennon and McCartney. I do, however, recall that when I first heard The Beatles' new album, '*Rubber Soul*', I was very disappointed. As a seven-year old, I obviously preferred the simple 'I love you, she loves me', pop song rather than the more sophisticated direction the band were taking. David took an interest in pop music in general and liked to write down the Top Thirty chart each week from the radio countdown or whilst watching Top of the Pops, something I would do myself in later life. We would annoy him some weeks by standing in the way of the television when they were doing a rundown of the charts and he was trying to write it down. That may be the reason that we three youngest children were not allowed to watch the 1966 World Cup Final on television but instead had to listen to it on the radio in another room. David regularly bought music magazines and had posters and information on his bedroom walls. Music and sport were very important to all the family. We did have some fun times with him as well as we used to have pillow fights and wrestling with him- three of us against one – and often referred to him as 'The Escaped Gorilla'. David had left school with no 'O' Levels but went on a catering course at Hereford Technical College. Eventually he got a job as a chef at the Feathers Hotel in Ledbury and moved out of home to live at the hotel. After that we only saw him on occasional visits home. Working in the kitchen meant David was engaged pretty much every day of the week.

Despite being poor, we did employ a housekeeper to come into our home once or twice a week to do the cleaning. With hindsight, that would suggest that maybe Dad was providing some money towards the upkeep of his family. I would like to say that our housekeeper, Miss Baldwin, was a lovely kind, old lady, which indeed she was, but not to us at the time. We were told to keep our bedrooms tidy which we tried our best to do- some of the time. If we left any toys on the floor, Miss Baldwin would pick them up….and put them in the dustbin! Once when she had put some my favourite cars in the bin. I tried to rescue them only to be chased away by her. I did manage to retrieve them eventually and I still have them today.

Mum helped out with the Girl Guides or Rangers from time to time. One Remembrance Sunday, she took the family to the service at St Michael and All Angels Church in Ledbury. We three youngest children got quite bored and wanted to go home but Mum had to stay with the Guides. We decided we would walk the two miles home by ourselves. At one point I said we should cross the road, so we were facing oncoming traffic. I checked for traffic and crossed. Colin, who must have only been five or six years old, followed me but had not noticed that a car was coming. He was hit by the car and thrown forwards into the road. He was injured, though not too seriously, and was taken to hospital. The police went to the church to notify Mum about what had happened. The officer approached Mum, who was with Peta, with one of Colin's shoes in his hand and said, "Your son has been in a car accident". I am sure that her first thought on seeing the shoe was that he had been killed! Of course, we were very concerned that our little brother had been hurt in the accident but any sympathy we had for him soon disappeared a few days later when the driver of the car visited him at home. He had brought Colin lots of sweets and Colin didn't let us have any of them. I guess that was fair enough since it may have partly been our fault. Simon felt particularly guilty or, at least, he pretended to take some responsibility. From then on, when we did the quarter mile to walk to school, I was to walk in front followed by Colin with Simon bringing up the rear. Simon claimed that would be the best way to keep Colin safe. Just to make sure he carried a stick or branch which he used on Colin to keep him in line and to remind him that his big brother was 'looking after him'.

Eastnor V.C. School was a very small primary school with just two classes. There was a class at one side of the school for the Infants and another class at the other side for the Juniors. In between was a large hall. I made a poor start to my career there when one of the older boys told me to ride on the gate at the entrance to the school grounds. I swung across the gap, holding on to the gate. This was against the school rules, not that I knew as I had only been there a few days, and I was caught. That misdemeanour led to my first, and thankfully only, experience of corporal punishment. I was whacked with the cane three times across the palm of my hand. Although it stung quite a lot, as soon as me and my accomplice were out of the room, we couldn't stop laughing. Another memorable incident was when one of the large classroom windows was hit by a football during morning break. Playing football in the schoolyard was one of the highlights of the day but the strike had left a large crack across the window. We were therefore banned from playing football. Later that day, at lunchtime, we were milling around with nothing to do, now we couldn't play football. One of the boys, Marcus Mortimer, suggested that we pretend to play football instead. With that, he swung his leg and shouted, 'Charlton whacks to ball into the back of the net'. Charlton's shot was so powerfully struck that his shoe came off and hit the same window that had been hit that morning making the crack even worse!

When the family had lived in Germany, they used to go on camping holidays. We still had a rather large tent from those days, so we continued the tradition. We could not afford to go on real holidays anymore so instead we would go to the nearby Eastnor Deer Park and pitch the tent there. Our school friends would join us and we spent some wonderful nights under the stars by a campfire. We enjoyed the freedom of doing as we pleased without any parents telling us what to do. There were the occasional problems such as leaky tents and being woken up by a cow sticking its nose into the tent and licking our butter! The park itself was near to Eastnor Castle, a nineteenth century folly which was built in the typical sandcastle design with a gatehouse and a tower in each of its four corners. The castle overlooked a large lake which was excellent for fishing though it required a licence to do so. Needless to say, lots of illegal fishing went on as there was plenty of cover from trees around the lake. Simon was especially keen on angling, but I did not have to patience to sit and stare at a float all day hoping something would bite.

Despite never having a proper holiday, we did go a few day trips. We joined Sunday School a couple weeks before there was a trip to Evesham which meant we were able to go. It was a real adventure to go on a coach to somewhere new and I enjoyed going on the paddle boats. After we got back, I don't think we went to Sunday School again.

David had moved on from his job at The Feathers and now worked at the Red Lion in Chipping Norton in Oxfordshire. David continued to give us an 'annual' book, usually based on a comic like The Dandy, for both our birthday and at Christmas. Given that we did not get many presents, getting a book was always a highlight of the day, unwrapping the parcel wondering which annual David had bought this time. When Peta got married in November 1968, David was invited but decided he did not want to attend. That was the last time we heard from him for many years. He cut himself off from the family and we did not know why.

It was now 1995, over thirteen years after the revelation that Mum and Dad had never married, and we were no nearer solving the mystery. Simon decided that we should make a concerted effort to trace David by starting with the last place we knew he was at. I had kept a diary from 1969 until the present day – though I lost 1972 and 1974 somewhere! It was quite interesting to read through my entries in them though they tended to be quite factual rather than revealing much about my emotions. On studying the diaries at the time, I found a comment in 1969 stating that 'Mum got £2 from Dad' and, in 1970, 'Dad sent £10 to Mum'. I was really heartened to realise that Dad had not completely abandoned us but was still providing some support for Mum. The 1970 diary also revealed that David was still sending me an annual for my birthday and we also had an address for him at The Bell in Charlbury, Oxfordshire. The diary suggested that, although we had seen nothing of David for a few years, he was still in contact with us though that was not to last much longer. The Bell manager was not able to tell us

where David had relocated to after his employment with them had ended, so our next strategy was to scour telephone directories for a D. I. Lovering. We found some D. Loverings and tried contacting them but could not find

David. Simon got a friend to help with the search and he came up trumps. David was now living in Canterbury in Kent. We contacted him. He appeared happy to hear from us and we arranged to visit him.

It was 5th February 1995 when Colin collected Peta, Simon and me to make the long drive from Herefordshire to Kent. None of us was sure what to expect or what we were going to say. Did David know anything about what happened between Mum and Dad? Did he know what had happened to Marie Cremin? There was also our theory that maybe he was a child of Dad and Marie and that Mum was not his true mother. When Mum and Dad separated, he had no real reason to feel attached to us. On the way to Canterbury, we stopped in Sittingbourne to visit Cryalls House where we had lived over thirty years before. I was only six years old when I last left there in the minibus, minus a cat, and thought the house was much smaller than I had always imagined it. The drive did not seem long after all and the monkey puzzle tree had been cut down.

I was able to visit the house again many years after our Canterbury trip. This time, because I wanted to take photos, I knocked on the door to let the owner know what I was doing. He was delighted to find out that I had lived there as he had written a book about the history of the house. I was not able to give him much extra information as I was so young when I lived there but he confirmed that it was often let to military families. The thrill for me, however, was that I was allowed into the house to have a look around. It appeared smaller than I remembered but that was no surprise really. Some extra internal walls had been erected to enclose the long staircase. I was led up those stairs to the attic rooms and able to enter the mysterious locked room. The owner explained that furniture, including some pictures, had been stored in there whilst the house had been rented out. No treasure after all. Slightly disappointing!

Back to our journey to see David in 1995. We left Sittingbourne to continue our journey to Canterbury. We managed to locate David's home. David lived in a rather small flat and the four of us waited in great anticipation as the door opened and he greeted us. The thing that struck me straight away was how much he looked like Mum. There was no doubt that Mum was his true mother and the theory that the real Marie was his mother could now be dismissed. The other noticeable thing was that the flat was quite sparse apart from a significant number of videos. It was probably all a little overwhelming for him as he was suddenly confronted with four siblings he had not seen for a quarter of a century. We took some photos and showed him some family pictures to help tell him the story of what had happened to us in the intervening years. David informed us that he was now the manager of a record shop in Canterbury. The years of reading music magazines and watching *Top of the Pops* had led him into a career in the music industry. He had also worked in record shops in other places including Southend where had become good friends with Depeche Mode. His record shop was one of the 'returns' shops for the company that compiled the UK weekly pop charts. The record companies knew where the shops were so would offer incentives to the shop managers to stock their product. Occasionally the artists themselves would visit the shop to promote their latest release in the hope of generating enough sales to get into the charts. That might then lead to an appearance for the artist on BBC's *Top of the Pops* and garner even more sales. David had rubbed shoulders with many stars including Donny Osmond and Kim Wilde. Just prior to our visit he had been involved in a nasty incident when he was mugged on the way home from work. Fortunately, he was all right physically but it had clearly knocked him back a little.

After an hour or so we said our goodbyes and started on the long journey home. We weren't quite sure what to make of the experience though we agreed that David appeared to be living a relatively solitary life at home but clearly enjoyed his work. We also realised that in the excitement of meeting him again that we had not directly asked him about Mum and Dad so had not found out what he knew. We were also a little sad that Bob had not been able to come as it would have been great for all six children to be together again. Sadly, that was never ever going to happen. We did not keep in contact with David and he made no effort to contact us. Poor communication between family members seemed to be a trait of the Lovering family over the years. As it happened, it would be another twenty years before we were in contact with David again.

4 BOB

Bob was the second eldest of the children and being only sixteen months younger than David, he would certainly have more recollections of Mum and Dad than any of the rest of us. When Simon first told him that Mum had confessed to not being married to Dad, he had expressed some surprise. However, he appeared quite reluctant to speculate about what the truth would be and did not seem as keen as the rest of us to talk about it. Bob was, in fact, the last member of the family to see Dad. In the final few years of his life, Dad had gone to live in Malta with his second wife, Claire. Bob had taken his family out to visit them but, when he returned, he would say little about the visit. The only detail of the trip I can recall him telling me was about the wonderful natural formation, the Blue Grotto, where you were taken in a boat along the coast into caves and under arches where the water was a sparkling azure blue colour. He said nothing about Dad. We wondered whether he knew more about Mum and Dad than he was willing to tell us.

Christopher John Lovering was born on 23rd September 1949 in Surrey like his older brother David. It was David that called him Bobby, as he could not say 'baby', and the name stuck. Also, just as David had done, Bob was sent to a private school whilst Dad was being posted by the Army to different places. Bob, however, attended Wolvestone Hall, near Ipswich in Suffolk. After finishing at Ipswich, he returned to live at home with us in Eastnor and went on to get further qualifications at Hereford Technical College. He was quite gifted academically though his major strength was in Art.

We three youngest children used to enjoy his company a lot as he would be very happy to join us in play activities. At Eastnor, there was a large field next to our house which sloped down from the woods down to the main road. Luckily there a flattish stretch about halfway down the hill on which we were able to play football. It was 1967 and Tottenham had just won the F.A. Cup, so Simon and I usually played as Spurs against Bob and Colin. They played as Ipswich Town as Bob had been to school there. We even made some goalposts from straight branches we found in the wood. Many happy hours were spent playing on that field, but the only problem was when the ball went off the flat section and rolled down the hill. It was a good opportunity to have a rest as we sent Colin down to fetch the ball! Colin, being the youngest, was often taken advantage off, or left out of the games altogether, if we wanted to be mean. Simon and I used to pretend to be secret agents called Mike and Jim, a little like Napoleon Solo and Ilya Kuryakin from '*The Man from UNCLE*', which was a popular TV series at the time. Colin also had random bit parts in our pretend adventures, often the baddie, and basically had to do as we told him.

Eventually, we did give him his own personal character, Chips, at least for a little while. One day, when Simon and I were in the bath playing with some boats, we were re-enacting an adventure involving Mike and Jim and their pal, Chips. Unfortunately, the boat that Chips was on got blown up and sunk. They were unable to save Chips. The next time we played with Colin we had to inform him that Chips was dead. You could say, 'he had had his chips'.

A common trait of all the members of the Lovering family was our sense of humour. I guess it was an antidote to some of the difficult times we had to live through. We were able to find some humour in almost any situation and Bob was particularly adept at coming out with a hilarious comment or amusing story. He had been raised on a healthy dose of '*The Goon Show*', '*Round The Horn*' and '*Hancock's Half Hour*'. One of our cats was called Eccles Bluebottle Goon by Bob though everyone just called the cat, Menace. Bob also gave us nicknames although I have no idea where he got mine from. He called me Oodi-ook-frey, whilst Simon was known as Tosh. I'm not sure what Colin's nickname was, that is if he had one. As I have hinted at previously, and Colin, himself, referred to it in a later wedding speech, he was often the odd-one-out. Occasionally, making witty comments can cause offence but the only time I think that Bob put his foot in it was when he literally did that. He had been poking around in the loft when he put his foot through the ceiling. Fortunately, it was his own bedroom ceiling so no-one else had to suffer having a draught during the night. I was to replicate the action when walking on the weak corrugated roof of the garage. I was like Bob in many ways, and he was a big influence on all of us.

We also had a lot of fun with Bob's friends over the years including Dusty, Klaus, Jon, Mace and Duck! It was the late sixties and music and fashion played a large part in young peoples' lives. Some of Bob's friends considered themselves to be 'mods' and had the Lambretta scooters to go with their love of mod clothes. One of the most terrifying experiences of my life was when Dusty offered to give me a ride on his scooter. I rode pillion down our very bumpy drive and the scooter was slipping all over the place on the loose surface. We were very fond of Dusty and he seemed to enjoy playing with us young kids. He would even let us play with his guitar.

Like David, and indeed all of us really, Bob loved his music. He was more into what became known as progressive music rather than the hits of the Top Thirty. Between them, the family had a wide range in tastes in their music which certainly had an impact on me, although I never really appreciated Mum's favourites, Johnny Ray and Sacha Distel! Bob got a good set of exam results at Hereford Technical College and qualified to commence a course on Art at Bournemouth College of Technology. That took him away from home once again, although only for a short while, as he did not complete the course.

In May 1969 we left The Gables in Eastnor and moved to more modest accommodation in nearby Ledbury. I assume the cost of renting the large house in Eastnor was too much to afford. Sadly, we did not leave the house and gardens in a good state. None of us were gardeners and the grass on the lawns had been allowed to mature into a mini jungle. The only digging we did was to bury a load of tin cans in the orchard area of the back garden. I have no idea why we did this. Was it because they stopped collecting our rubbish so we started our own landfill site or did we hope that by planting the cans, they would germinate and produce more food? Probably the only improvement we made to The Gables was cleaning out the old pigsty, a sturdy brick building, and turning it into a fantastic den to play in.

We found ourselves in a new dwelling at 2A, High Street in Ledbury. It was next to the famous Market House and above a baker's shop. There was no garden at all this time and the door opened out directly onto the High Street, so no long drive to walk up either. Ledbury is quite a small town, so it was still quite easy to get into the countryside, with Dog Hill Wood just a few minutes walk away. Living in a town meant we also had shops and streets to explore so we could have different sorts of adventures. I only had a couple of months left at Eastnor School. It was decided that I should continue to attend school there, catching the old Bristol Green bus each day. Colin, however, went to Ledbury Junior School and Simon was already a pupil of Ledbury Secondary Modern School so he was now able to walk to school.

Bob was living back home with us now after dropping out of college and 'Back Home' played a part in another infamous family occasion. 'Back Home' was the Number One hit single of the England Football team which was playing in the 1970 World Cup in defence of the title won in 1966. England had given favourites Brazil a run for their money before losing by the only goal scored in the group stage match. It was expected that England and Brazil would meet again in the Final, but first England had to get past West Germany in the Quarter-Final. Goalkeeper Gordon Banks was missing the game due to food poisoning but when England went 2-0 up, no-one was worried about Peter Bonetti replacing him. Sir Alf Ramsey even took Bobby Charlton off to save him for the Semi-Final as he thought the game was won. Germany then scored and then got another goal, the equaliser. We realised that Bonetti was nicknamed

'The Cat' because he made a paw goalkeeper! It was at this point that Simon started supporting West Germany, since he had been born there. This change of support did not please Bob at all. When Germany scored the winner, Bob finally lost his temper and threw the teapot at Simon. He missed Simon, but the teapot smashed. England were out of the Cup, but it did not matter as we had no tea to put in it. If the pot had hit Simon, he might have been seeing stars. As it was, he could still see stars because Bob and his friends had helped to decorate the living room by painting the ceiling black and sticking gold and silver stars on it!

We had a visit from some old friends of the family whilst we lived in Ledbury. Uncle Bob and Auntie Barbara came with their two daughters, Jane and Susan, and stayed a few days. At the time, we just thought they were old friends of Mum but, with the mystery of who Mum really was, it could be that they were really blood relatives.

Maybe Mum is really Helen Lenham, or whatever Barbara's maiden name was!

A long running joke in the house was that Mum would often ask Bob what he wanted for tea the following evening. It went something like this:

Mum: "What do you want for tea tomorrow, Bob?"

Bob: "Cucumber jelly!"

Mum: "Oh, do be sensible."

Bob: "I am being sensible. I want cucumber jelly!"

Bob would always be disappointed when he came home from work and Mum served him fish cakes and chips (usually burned!). One day, Mum decided to surprise him and made a cucumber jelly. It was not the familiar sweet jelly that we usually had as a pudding, but a jelly made from aspic or something like that. It tasted so awful, that that was the end of the 'cucumber jelly' response.

A peculiarity of the house in the High Street was that it could pick up a variety of regional television channels. It might have been because we had a clear sight from our window of the television transmitter at Much Marcle. Whatever the reason, it meant we were to become quite popular with friends of Bob. '*Monty Python's Flying Circus*' had just begun transmission, but it was not shown across all the networks. The local BBC station did not broadcast the show, but it was on another regional network that we could receive. Consequently, each week, a group of Bob's friends would descend for the ritual of watching this very silly and unusual comedy programme. Naturally we all stayed up late to watch it as well and its off-the-wall humour certainly resonated with all of us brought up on *The Goon Show* and the wit of Bob. Another strange phenomenon was that we could listen to the audio of some television programmes on the radio so if we were sent to bed when a favourite programme was on, we might be able to, at least, listen to it under the bed clothes.

One of the most exciting things to happen whilst we lived in Ledbury was when Hollywood came to nearby Eastnor Castle. The film was to be called '*One More Time*' and starred Sammy Davis Jr and Peter Lawford and was being directed by Jerry Lewis. Many of the stars were staying at The Feathers Hotel so were often seen coming and going around Ledbury. Mum was particularly thrilled when Sammy Davis Jr leaned out of his taxi and said 'hello' to her with a big smile on his face. Some of the Rat Pack was in Ledbury. It was hard to believe! Simon, Colin and I went over to Eastnor to see some of the filming take place and to chat with the stars and the crew. I had a cricket bat so we would often play with the largely English film crew between takes, using a paper cup for a ball. Some of the American stars took an interest and one day, Jerry Lewis took the bat and asked about cricket and what it was all about. It was a real thrill to be mingling with the stars and I got them to sign my bat as well. Sadly, the film itself was not particularly good and not a big hit but it was interesting to view the scenes that we had witnessed being filmed. There was another touch of Hollywood in Eastnor, but it was for the future. The star in question was only ten years old at the time. Amazingly, I had actually gone to school with a Hollywood film star. The ten-year old girl was Rebecca de Mornay, who later starred in films including '*Risky Business*' (with Tom Cruise, who became her boyfriend for while) and '*The Hand That Rocks The Cradle*'. Her mum was taking her two children, Rebecca and younger brother Peter, round Europe. She only attended Eastnor School for a few months, but I was probably one of her best friends. That was because I had a map of California and was really interested about her home in the USA. She showed me where she had lived, in Pasadena, and what it was like in America compared with rural Herefordshire. I often wonder whether she still remembers me!

Bob got a job working in Harry Isaacs, a betting shop in Hereford, and eventually found somewhere to live in Tupsley, a suburb of Hereford. His home was known to us as the 'Hippy House' as it was occupied by very long-haired young men who liked playing progressive music and there was always a certain aroma around the whole house. I was, of course, too young to recognise all the smells and thought that they just burned a few joss sticks. Working in a betting shop meant Bob encountered a wide variety of characters including footballers from the local professional team, newly elected into the Football League, Hereford United, as well as various musicians. Some of them would become successful in their careers including a member or two of the band Mott The Hoople. I would sometimes visit Bob at the shop and he would allow me to bet on a greyhound race or horse race after giving me some tips. Bob became very knowledgeable about the runners and riders, often hearing of rumours on the grapevine or patterns in the betting which suggested that there might be something awry. It was strange that Bob ended up the racing expert as it had been older brother, David, that had come to the attention of the National press when he successfully backed the winner of the Grand National a few years in a row. This was made even more remarkable by the fact that one of his winners was Foinavon in the famous race of 1967 when many horses fell at the same fence. Foinavon stayed on his feet and came in first with odds of 100/1. I should add that I had the horse that came in second that day so you could say that picking the right horse 'ran' in the family. Not far from the Bob's bookmakers' shop was Buzz Music, the haven in Hereford for collectors of good music, selling both new and second-hand records- just vinyl in those days. It was a place I would visit every time I made the fourteen-mile rail journey to Hereford. It was not very easy to buy records in Ledbury. The local branch of Woolworths stocked the chart albums and singles but little else. If you wanted a release by a more obscure artist, you had to order it specially from Lacy's, an electrical shop. There was always a sense of great excitement when you went to collect your record, particularly when you finally had it in your hands and could study the sleeve. Perusing the record sleeves in Buzz Music was an enlightening experience. Many of the artists in the late sixties and early seventies had wonderful artwork on the sleeves even though I had no idea what the music inside was like. It was only when I began to watch the late-night BBC television programme, *The Old Grey Whistle Test*, that I began to hear some of the music of those artists.

Some of it was good and some was, shall we say, very interesting.

During this time, Bob met and married Janet Morris. The wedding was a bit of a secret affair with only Mum invited from the family. Simon got wind of it and attended at the registry office with his girlfriend at that time. Colin was living with Mum, so he was there as well. Peta and I did not find out until days later that Bob and Jan had got married. At least this was a family secret that was not kept very long! It was in the move from the Hippy House in Tupsley to his new home with Jan that the biscuit tin of family photos and documents was left behind and lost forever. The picture of Mum at Bob's wedding is probably the earliest photo that we have left of her. Were there any photos or documents in the tin that might have revealed a little more of the truth? We will never find out but maybe Bob knew what was in the tin.

Bob later got a job working in a menswear shop, G. Alfred, near the cathedral in Hereford. Many of the clientele he encountered at the bookies were now able to take his advice on the latest fashions and we were able to benefit from a reduced price. Occasionally Simon and I would meet Bob at lunchtime to go to the nearby putting greens by the river Wye. Although the games were only meant to be for fun, they were often hotly contested. Golf would become a big part of Simon's life many years later. Bob always fancied himself as a good golfer and cricketer and would often tell tales of his fine deeds. I once visited his house to see Jan and Tim. Bob invited me to have a go with his practice driving ball It was a plastic ball full of holes that could be hit hard but would not travel far. Bob went first and hit a good shot then I followed it with a perfect shot. It was only a fluke but that was the end of practice driving as Bob did not like being shown up! Another time he was telling me how well his quiz team had been the previous evening. He was saying how he was the only one who knew the Japanese name for a tidal wave. I replied 'What, a tsunami?'. He was a little deflated that I knew the answer so just corrected my pronunciation and quickly moved on to another subject.

Despite not being particularly wealthy, Bob and Jan had Tim privately educated and he was very successful academically, ultimately achieving a PhD at university. History was his subject, I believe, and he later became an archivist, but he was particularly interested in military history. He was naturally curious about what both his grandfathers had done during the Second World War and so obtained their service records and other documents. He often made contributions to a magazine called '*Practical Family History*' and he published his findings about Reg Morris, Janet's dad, and Arthur Lovering in an edition in 2009.

All we knew about Dad's wartime experience was that he was in the Royal Artillery and been involved in the Italian campaign so reading Tim's account was fascinating. Earlier documents confirmed that Dad had been a merchant seaman from 1929 until 1935 having attended the Royal Hospital School in Greenwich from 1925 to 1928 where he passed the Naval School Examination. This demonstrated his strength in statistics which would be a huge part of his later life with the Ministry of Defence working in Manpower Statistics. This strength was clearly passed on to both myself and my eldest son, Tom. We both did university degrees in mathematics. Serving time at sea was expected of pupils of the Royal Hospital School which is probably why he became a merchant seaman. Prior to the War, Dad had been progressing as an estate agent, but he was enlisted on 17th October 1940 as a clerk in the Royal Army Ordnance Corps. He trained with the ROAC's No 4 Training Battalion before being promoted to acting lance-corporal and being posted to Portsmouth before sailing to Egypt in January 1942. There he remained with 2 Base Workshops, obtaining various certificates and promotion to corporal, before being transferred to the Royal Electrical and Mechanical Engineers where he became a sergeant. He was also trained in gunnery and became an instructor with the Royal Artillery. He remained in Egypt until he was posted to an Officer Cadet Training Unit in August 1943. After he was commissioned, he sailed for Italy where he served with 178 Medium Regiment of the Royal Artillery until 1945. This would suggest that our memory of him telling stories of being at the siege of the monastery at Monte Cassino could well be true. Dad returned home at the end of the War, but it wasn't long before he was heading east to spend nine months with a unit of the Royal Indian Artillery. He then continued to work in the army until relinquishing his commission in 1963 and working for the Ministry of Defence until retirement.

One interesting point from this information was that Dad

had married Marie Cremin in December 1932 when he was supposedly a merchant seaman, yet his marriage certificate lists him as a hotel waiter. Maybe he was ashore for some time so did hotel work to keep some money coming in whilst he waited for another job on a ship. Marie possibly got fed up with him being away at sea, so he gave up on the travelling away from home and worked on trading homes instead, as an estate agent.

Given that David was born in May 1948, Dad must have known Mum before August 1947 suggesting that they probably met after he had returned from his stint with the Royal Indian Artillery. If only Mum had told us a bit more about what she had done after the War then we might have a clue as to how they met. She, of course, maintained that she was Marie Cremin. I am quite certain she did not say that she had been married for seven years before the Second World War had even begun! She had admitted that she had lied about her age to get in the services. She would have been a child to get married in 1932. All three of the eldest children were born in Surrey or London so Dad must have been based at home until the family moved out to West Germany prior to Simon's birth in 1955. We wondered whether there may be men from his battalion still alive who might know how he came to meet mum. Even if there were, it would be virtually impossible to trace them. It would be quite good just to find any photos of Dad with his fellow comrades.

Tim's article was written long after Dad had died but Tim had visited Malta with Bob when he was a child. I wondered whether Tim had talked to Dad about his military experiences. I am certain that Bob would have had conversations with Dad about the past. Did they talk about Mum and the family as well? It would be very strange if they did not. Did Bob know more about Mum's true background?

5 PETA

Being the only daughter, Peta was probably closer to Mum than any of the rest of the children and was also old enough to have known Dad much better that me. I always found it quite amusing when anyone asked if I had any brothers or sisters. I would reply: 'Yes, four brothers and a sister called Peta'. The listener would not know how Peta was spelt so just assumed that my parents really wanted another son. As it was, the story went that after having their third child Peta, Mum and Dad decided they would have no more children. They managed that for four years before the three of us 'young ones' arrived. Peta was an unusual name, I have no idea where my parents got that name from, but her middle name is Helen which I believed was Mum's real name. When the mystery of Mum's identity was first raised with Peta, she reacted in much the same way that Bob had done. She showed a little surprise but did not share our curiosity and desire to find out the truth. In fact, there was a situation where she may have, probably accidently, prevented us discovering something. Simon had visited Mum one evening and proceeded to ply her with whisky and any other alcohol to hand. She was beginning to loosen up her conversation and Simon believes she was on the verge of revealing her true identity. At that moment, Peta arrived at the house and the chance was gone. Peta was always very protective of Mum and discouraged us from asking Mum about her past lest it might upset her.

Peta Helen Lovering was born on 23rd November 1951 in Kensington, London. Unlike David and Bob, she did not enjoy the privilege of an education at a boarding school. Instead, she went to the local secondary modern school, first in Sittingbourne and then in Ledbury. She left school at fifteen with few, if any, qualifications and got a job working at The Wellington Inn, which was a few miles from Ledbury, at Chances Pitch on the road to Malvern. Although she was living at home throughout this time, I have few memories of her being there as we did not tend to play with her at all. There were times when she would annoy us and we used to, rather cruelly, call her Fanny Fishface. Like David and Bob, she was keen on the music of the time and would occasionally travel to Birmingham to see the music programme hosted by Brian Matthew, '*Thank Your Lucky Stars*', being recorded for television. Like many teenage girls of the time, she was after a little bit of her music heroes and she once got the remains of Keith Moon's drumstick and the shoelace of Dave Dee, or was it of Dozy, Beaky, Mick or Titch?

It was whilst working at The Wellington Inn that she met Stephen Barnes. It was not long before they announced that they were to get married. The marriage was to take place at Eastnor Church on Peta's seventeenth birthday on 23rd November 1968. The wedding would be a big occasion for the family as Peta was the first of the Lovering children to get married, but there were a few problems. Firstly, it was tradition for the bride's family to fund a wedding and our financial situation meant that would be very difficult. It is also traditional for the bride to be given away by her father. Mum and Dad's relationship was long over but it was still very disappointing that Dad did not want to come to his only daughter's big day. The alternative to Dad giving her away could be that her eldest brother could perform the duty. David, however, had also become estranged from the family so he too would not attend. The next choice was the next eldest brother and Bob manfully stepped into the role and the day was a huge success. I must admit that I do not remember much of it. Colin was a page boy and the reception was at The Horse And Jockey pub in Colwall. I was bought a suit to wear for the day which then became my school clothes for the last few months at Primary School. Steve's mother was a Jehovah's Witness so I do not know her feelings about a wedding with a Church of England ceremony.

Steve worked on a farm and, after living initially near Colwall, they moved to a house in Hanley Castle. The house had views of the Malvern Hills and was opposite the farm where Steve worked. The house came with the job. Peta gave birth to a daughter, Mum's first grandchild, in June 1969. Claudette Marie Barnes was named after her grandmother though we now know that she is really named after Dad's first wife! Two years later, Paul Simon Barnes, was born and I thought it strange that Peta gave birth to him at home, though I do not know why as it was quite common in those days. I should also have not been surprised as Steve would often return home from work having helped with the birth of a calf or two. His wife having a baby upstairs at home should have felt quite natural. Mum was at the house for the birth and, despite his experience with farm animals, it was still a nervous time for Steve that evening.

Although Hanley Castle was a small place in the middle of nowhere, we would often go to stay with Peta and Steve. As we were very poor, we never had real holidays so going to stay somewhere else was quite exciting. We would often walk to Hanley Castle from Ledbury, or, at least, part of the way which was nothing to us even though it was about twelve miles. We often used to go for long walks, usually for no reason apart from the fact we wanted to do a long walk. On one occasion, we planned a seventeen mile walk just so we could 'walk off the map'. It was quite exciting when we left the edge of our Ordnance Survey map, found the road junction, turned right and, a few moments later, appeared back on the map. Who needed holidays at the seaside or in Spain with that level of entertainment on the doorstep, or just off the map! The stays at Hanley Castle also provided the experience of living with a farm worker. Steve would bring a chicken home from work and we would have to help Peta prepare it for dinner which would involve having to pluck it first. Steve was very tolerant having his wife's brothers about when all he wanted when he got home from work was his tea on the table, to peruse the racing results and relax in front of the television. I think he enjoyed the occasional games of football or cricket in the garden and, looking back, I must thank Steve and Peta for giving us a break from living at home.

We were still living in the heart of the small market town of Ledbury. Mum was now working at The Hereford Bull, a steak house just up the road, run by a Hungarian refugee from the war. As well as being more convenient to get to than the journey Mum had had to get to Malvern College, working there also meant we were able to enjoy steak for tea a few times each week. It was still a real struggle to put food on the table otherwise and Mum often had no money left to feed us. We would sometimes go out hunting for discarded Corona bottles around the town. There was a deposit paid on the glass bottles when people bought them. If we could find any, we could return them to the shop and claim the money back. I was now attending Ledbury Grammar School and enjoyed the fact that it was only a five-minute walk away from home. Simon was growing up fast and enjoying the company of girls more and more. Bob was at home occasionally, but we had got used to not having a dominant male figure around, some of us never having experienced having a father, but all that was about to change.

In July 1970, Mum was out one evening attending a party. This was quite a rarity as Mum would usually be working if she was not at home in the evening. Not long after that evening, Mum announced that she had a new boyfriend and that she would introduce us to him. The following day, Michael Roy Barnes came to the house to visit us. He bought us ice creams so our first impression of him was very good. He must have felt comfortable with us too, as he moved in two days later! Mike was quite a bit younger than Mum and had originally grown up in the Black Country in the Midlands. He was a follower of The Baggies, a nickname for the football team West Bromwich Albion. I had not heard them called that before. He had a very slight build, smoked a pipe, told us of his experiences in the Korean War and seemed like a nice bloke. I think he was a truck driver at the time that he and Mum got together. Mum obviously had not told him of her past because he questioned why everyone called her Helen when that was not her real name. From now on, he would call her Marie.

It was quite strange having a father figure in the house after spending most of my life with only a mother and siblings at home. Mike had his own ideas about how things should be and there was friction between us on many occasions, although I think he was trying very hard to fit in with the family. Once he got fed up with us playing football in the hallway, so he cut the football in half with a knife. For us football was now, literally, a game of two halves! He set up his own little workshop in the hallway area at the bottom of the building where he began his business as an electrical repair man. He even had a contract repairing Scalextric cars with Tilleys, the local, well-known stationery and toyshop. We all thought that having Mike around, and in work, would mean that we would now be a little better off financially but that was not always the case. There were many times when I did not have my dinner money because Mike had 'not been paid yet'. It may have been the nature of the jobs he did which meant that income was intermittent, but it turned out that he also spent his money on other things, namely alcohol, which was to blight his life.

Just after only two months of moving in, Mum and Mike got married on 26th September 1970 so, in the space of two years, two members of the Lovering family had become Mrs Barnes! The wedding itself was quite an event as our small home was invaded by friends of Mum and Mike as well as some of Bob's mates. I was only twelve years old at the time so was a little bewildered by the amount of alcohol and jollity that there was. I woke up quite early the following morning and had to carefully step over various bodies as I made my way round the house. There was talk of us children having to change our surname to Barnes as well. There was no way I wanted to do that and said that I would change it back to Lovering as soon as I was eighteen years old. Nothing happened and, happily, I remained a Lovering.

The wedding had been preceded by another big event in the family when Mike got a car, a Hillman Husky. It was the first time that there been a car in the family since Dad lived with us. Steve had owned an Austin A40 which was useful for Peta and her family. Mike took Simon and Colin for a ride in the car when he first brought it home which made me feel jealous, as I was not around. The following day, he took us all for a day trip to Goodrich Castle and we had an enjoyable time. Maybe the quality of our lives was going to improve after all. However, that thought came crashing down, quite literally. Just two weeks after the wedding, Mike was involved in an accident and the car was written off. He had been drink-driving and it led to a court appearance, though I cannot recall what the outcome was. It was the first time we saw what effect alcohol was having on his life. Mike recognised that he had an issue with drinking and joined Alcoholics Anonymous but that was not going to solve his problem entirely.

Steve had left the farm in Hanley Castle and now worked on a farm nearer to his own parents in the small village of Colwall which nestled on the western side of the Malvern Hills. As before, the job came with a tied house, so Peta moved into Grovesend Cottage. It was a good-sized house which sat in amongst a mixture of factory units, domestic housing and a fruit processing depot. Colwall was only five miles from Ledbury, so it meant that Peta was closer to her family too. It presented more opportunities for Mum to enjoy the company of her grandchildren, Claudette and Paul. Claudette would call Mum her 'Granary'. I called Claudette, 'Clogbert'.

Life in Ledbury was generally good for us as we enjoyed having our friends living nearby. Many evenings were spent playing football on the Ledbury Town football ground, just kids having a kick about rather than organised games. The nets were often left up which made playing more enjoyable as you did not have to go and fetch the ball every time a goal was scored. We were frequently joined by Steven Emery who would later become a professional footballer for Hereford United and

Derby County. They were heady days for Hereford United who famously beat Newcastle United in the F.A. Cup Third Round with help from that Ronnie Radford goal. We would often also watch games at the Town ground which was adjacent to a cemetery. Each time the ball went over the wall of the cemetery, some wag (usually me) would shout 'dead ball!'. During a Cup game, a group of us decided that we would invade the pitch at the end of the game. The others later decided they would not bother but did not tell me. The final whistle was blown and I led the one man invasion carrying my umbrella. The rest of my friends were in fits of laughter. It was another rather embarrassing moment in my life.

To earn some money, we took on a paper round which I shared with Simon and Colin at various times. Mike had helped assemble a bike for me from odd bits of other bikes. The papers would arrive by bus and be deposited under The Market House, just outside our front door. Copies of Hereford Evening and Worcester Evening papers were delivered by us, and we collected the money from the houses. Every two or three weeks, the agent would call to collect the money for the papers and we would keep the profit. Unfortunately, the money that was collected was kept in a drawer and some had disappeared by the time the agent visited. I did not know who took the money. Given it was in the Lovering house, it could have been anyone! This meant that I did the paper round for virtually no reward but, at least, I enjoyed the evening rides on the bike. Living in rural Herefordshire also provided another way to get some pocket money as, every Summer, workers were required to pick fruit. For us that meant going blackcurrant picking in Wellington Heath or Hollybush. It was not an enjoyable task, and you were paid by the weight of a bucketful of blackcurrants. On a good day, I might pick five or six buckets and then a bit more fruit to take home to make our own version of the blackcurrant drink, Ribena. At night, after a day picking fruit, I would stink of blackcurrants. My hands would be stained a purple colour and, as soon as I closed my eyes, all I could see were blackcurrants! The weather was important as a hot, sunny day would be quite unbearable. Rain was not pleasant either, but the fruit was heavier, so you did not have to pick as much to get the same money.

The fair came to the main streets of Ledbury for two days every October and I think both Simon and Colin worked on the dodgems in some years. They supplemented their wages by checking for loose change which might have been dropped by customers in the cars. Of course, there was also the temptation of not giving the right change back to a customer, but I am sure that sort of thing never happened at the fair! The penny falls machines were another way of picking up some money as players would sometimes leave before realising some pennies had dropped. Giving the tables a strong nudge might also yield some coins. You had to be discrete to ensure you were not caught. Simon regularly attended the Army Cadet Force evenings and Mum and I would help out in the tuck shop. It did not pay me any money, but I did help myself to the odd bar of chocolate!

A rather strange thing happened a few months after her wedding when Mum announced that she might be having a baby. This took us completely by surprise as Mum must surely have been in her high forties by then. Having a father around the house was one thing but the thought of a baby Barnes as well would bring other problems! Mum did not have a baby, but I do not know why. Perhaps it was a false alarm or maybe there were problems with the pregnancy. Whatever the reason, nothing was said about it again.

Mike's drink problem caught up with him again in March 1971 when he did not return home one evening. It transpired that he had set fire to The Giffard Hotel in Worcester and had been arrested for arson. He was remanded in custody, initially in Gloucester Prison though he later transferred to Winson Green in Birmingham. It was a huge shock to all of us and a big blow for Mum who we thought had at last found some happiness after all the hard years of bringing us up on her own. She was very supportive of Mike and dutifully visited him whenever she could in the time leading up to his trial. He was in prison for two months until finally, at his trial which took place in Stafford, he was found guilty of arson and given two years on probation. He was released from prison and able to return home but would have to report to his probation officer regularly. Mike was lucky to get away with just that punishment as it could have been much more severe. Mum was obviously relieved to have him back home again.

A fresh start for Mike was needed and, before too long, he found himself a more permanent job which took him away from Ledbury. He would be a caretaker/handy man at a private school a few miles north of Worcester. The job was at Abberley Hall and came with a house as part of the salary. I was in the Fourth Year at Ledbury Grammar School and Mum did not want my education to be disrupted by a change of schools. Peta and Steve kindly agreed to let me move in with them at Colwall where I could get the bus into school. Colin had only just started at Ledbury Secondary Modern School, so it seemed less of a need for him to remain there. He moved into the new home at Abberley with Mum and Mike. Simon, by this time, had left home to join the army and to go on to other adventures.

The house at Abberley was rather idyllic as we had the run of the school grounds in the evenings, including use of the tennis courts. Colin attended The Chantry School in nearby Martley. Given the circumstances that surrounded the decision to make a new start, it is ironic that not far the school there were the ruins of a fine country mansion at Witley Court. It had been burned to the ground many years before. Mike was not responsible this time! I only visited during the holidays as it was not an easy journey to get there from Colwall, involving a train journey to Worcester then a bus out to Abberley. Our walking adventures continued and one day we made the trek to Ludlow and stayed at the Youth Hostel there. It felt like a proper holiday, even though we only stayed one night, because we were away from grown-ups. Unlike our camping breaks in Eastnor Park, it was also much more comfortable. My relationship with Mike, however, was quite strained. I guess I never really got used to having him around and only visiting occasionally somehow made it even more difficult. He got upset once when he felt our jokes about Mum somehow overstepped the mark although they were the sorts of comments we had always made. With hindsight, they may have been a little cruel at times, but that was part of the warped Lovering sense of humour. Mike probably never fully grasped that they were always made with affection. Colin, on the other hand, built up a close relationship with Mike whilst they lived at the school. With just him living with Mum and Mike, Mike was able to spend more time with Colin and share more stories and adventures with him. They would explore the school grounds and take unusual pictures of the trees. Mike, who could put his hand to most tasks, was able to share some of those skills with Colin. In many ways Colin was lucky as, for a while, he was able to experience what it was like to have a real father, something the rest of us did not have. Unfortunately, the happy family life was not to last and this time there would be even worse disruption to the family.

In September 1973, Mike hit the bottle again and this time he set fire to the school that he was paid to help maintain. He went on the run for a few days before returning to Mum who persuaded him to give himself up. Once again, he was remanded in custody so was back in prison. Another two months passed before his trial and this time he was not as lucky as before. He was sentenced to five years and three months at Her Majesty's pleasure. Mum continued to stand by him and would regularly go to visit him when she had the time and money to do so. That task was made even harder when he was transferred briefly to Wakefield Prison in Yorkshire in February 1975 before being moved to Dartmoor Prison. In August of that year, I went with Mum on the train to Plymouth where we caught a bus up to Yelverton on Dartmoor and checked into a Bed & Breakfast establishment. The following morning, we set off to visit Mike in Dartmoor Prison. It was a quite misty day and seeing the large grey building appear in the gloom ahead of us really brought it home to me what a desolate place it was. The moors surrounding the prison would not be very welcoming if anyone decided to try to escape from the prison. It was also quite depressing to see Mike in the visitors' room when we finally got through security and into the prison. He seemed so helpless and bereft of life and joy as he exchanged words with the two of us. We stayed another night and visited him the following day for the final time before we headed back on the long journey home. I risked my own freedom before we left as a stole some soap from the restroom. It somehow felt right to nick something from the nick.

The other consequence of Mike's actions that night at the school was, of course, that Mum and Colin could no longer live at the house and were homeless. Peta and Steve came to the rescue again and put them both up in the cottage in Colwall where I was living. It was only a temporary stay as Mum was able to secure a job at The Laurels, an old peoples' home in Bromsberrow, a few miles south of Ledbury. As with Abberley, there was some accommodation which came with the job, only this time, it was a small caravan in the grounds of the home. Colin went with Mum to live in the caravan, but I remained with Peta and Steve in Colwall. Colin had to move back to the Secondary School in Ledbury, another disruption to his schooling. He had to find his own way into Ledbury each morning to attend school. For a time, he had a bike but that got stolen, so he had to walk or hitch his way to and from school. Colin and Mum were very close living in the caravan, both physically and spiritually, as they spent many evenings passing the time playing cards or games of Scrabble. If only Colin had known then about Mum and Dad not being married. He could have had some interesting conversations with Mum about her early life to glean some information about her. Life must have been very tough for Mum then, with her husband in prison and the family split up and living all over the place. Colin said he had happy times in the caravan though the old people would complain that he was playing David Bowie's '*Jean Genie*' record too loud!

Mum had applied to the Ledbury Housing department to get a new home so the family could be re-united. Eventually they found a flat for us, in Lawnside Road in Ledbury, in early 1975. It was a two-bedroomed flat on the second, and top floor, of a council block. It was situated right next to the recreation ground, known locally as 'The Rec'. I packed my things in Colwall and was able to join Mum and Colin in the flat, sharing a bedroom with Colin again. It was good to have the family back together and, in April 1977, Mike was released from prison and came home too.

Mike was encouraged to regularly attend meetings of Alcoholics Anonymous on his return and he tried to find some secure employment. He did some truck driving again and I went with him on one trip. He was transporting a very wide load to somewhere near Peterborough. Mike should really have asked for a police escort but did not. We navigated our way eastwards across the country following the maps. No satnavs in those days! Unfortunately, a low bridge was not indicated on the map and we were unable to pass under it. The police were required after all. I found it quite a thrill to be in the cab of a big lorry with a police escort clearing the traffic out of the way for us. Later, he got another job operating a digger on building sites. Once again, I spent a day with him at work when he was involved in the construction of an underground reservoir in Aconbury, near Hereford. Mike eventually got a 'steady' job as a travelling salesman, which took him away from home again and touring round the country. He was selling novelty items such as amusing, but sometimes risqué, posters to shops, usually in holiday resorts.

During this time, Peta and Steve became parents of a third child, a son, James. He was named after me (my middle name) and I was his godfather. I had left the Grammar School in Ledbury and gone to the University of York to study for a degree in Mathematics and Education. After graduating, I stayed on in York for another year to train as a mathematics teacher. Before I started the course, I had got a phone call from my old school, which, by now, had become a comprehensive school, asking if I wanted a job there. I explained that I had not completed my training yet so could not accept the offer. The following year they rang again and this time I was able to take up the post. I started teaching at The John

Masefield High School in September 1980. The old Grammar School buildings were now used for the Junior Department of the school. It was very strange indeed to now be a teacher and enter the hallowed staff room where my old teachers were now my colleagues. The advantage of moving back home again meant I would, hopefully, be able to build up some savings so I could then buy a home of my own in the future. Colin, by this time, had got married and moved out so I had the bedroom to myself. Mike had built a workshop for himself in the small spare room in the Lawnside Road flat which he kindly cleared for me to use when I started work. Mike was not at home that much with travelling, so did not really need the space anymore. Family life was stable for a change but that was not to last for very long.

By June 1981, I was near the end of my first year of teaching and had got into the routine of spending the evenings marking books and preparing lessons whilst listening to my records. Most weekends I was either involved in Saturday morning school sporting fixtures or visiting my girlfriend, Pauline East, in York. Mum had got a job at Priory Cleaners, a dry-cleaning shop in The Homend in Ledbury. One evening after tea, the phone rang. I answered it. It was Mike and I asked if he wanted to speak to Mum. He said no and then said, "You'll be able to look after Mum now. I'm not coming home. I'm going to live in southern Ireland" and with that he hung up. I went to tell Mum who appeared surprised but took it rather well. I think we both could not quite believe what had just happened. It took a while for the news to sink in. Mike was leaving Mum and not coming home again.

Mum must have been hurting deeply inside having stood by his side during his times in prison only to be deserted by him. Just when it seemed, at last, that things were going well in her life for a change, this bombshell falls. Colin told me, many years later, that Mike's boss had been a bit of a tyrant and that he left Ledbury because he feared for his safety. If true, was Mum aware of the situation? Maybe she had been expecting Mike to take flight.

We both had to get on and try to cope without Mike. I was able to pay some of the bills even though it would mean not being able to save as much. Mum struggled on and got some joy from her new dog called Phoebe who was often referred to as the rat! I thought I had been paying the bills. I had given the money to Mum to pay them, but I was to discover that she did not! I came home in February 1982 to find the Midlands Electricity Board (M.E.B.) were threatening to cut us off as the bill for £240 had not been paid. I dug into my savings to pay it and tried not to make a big deal of it. I was not happy but recognised that Mum had problems. However, things were to get much worse. I got a phone call at work, a few weeks later, to say they were worried as Mum had not turned up for work. I rushed home to find Mum on the floor and an empty bottle of paracetamol tablets next to her. She was unconscious, but still alive. I dialled 999 to call an ambulance. I travelled with Mum in the ambulance to Hereford General Hospital where they were able to pump the tablets out of her stomach. They said she probably had not taken enough to kill herself, but it was a close-run thing. I left the hospital feeling quite numb and contacted

Bob and Simon to let them know what had happened. I asked them to tell Peta as well. I got soaked in a heavy shower on the way to catch the train back to Ledbury, but I had too much on my mind to be bothered about being wet. Mum remained in hospital several days and then went to stay for Peta for a while when she was allowed to leave. Over the days that followed, I discovered one of the reasons why she may have tried to take her life. The M.E.B. were asking for more money, £180 for the electricity bill and a further £180 as security. I also found out that Mum had borrowed £100 from Joyce whom she worked with at Priory Cleaners and had not paid her back. More of my savings went on settling those debts. I felt so frustrated that Mum had not been honest with me and should have paid the bills when I gave her the money. She could have asked to borrow from me if she needed more but I guess she felt it would be wrong to do that. I made sure that I paid the bills directly after that and tried to look after Mum and keep her spirits up once she returned home.

Mum suffered another loss later that year. It was 6th July and I had just finished marking some books in my room and was about to get ready for bed. Mum knocked on the door and said, 'Your father has died'. It was soon after Northern Ireland had beaten Spain in the World Cup. Maybe the excitement was too much for him. I should have felt something that my father had died but I had not known him at all, so hearing of his death did not affect me in any way. Yes, I was sad that he had passed away, but also sad for the fact that it had meant so little to me. It was around that time, in 1982, that Mum made the admission to Simon that she had not even been married to Dad.

The years passed and Mum seemed to be coping with life on her own. I had got a new job and had moved to Bristol to live with Pauline. We had two children and would regularly make the hour's drive up the motorway to visit Granny, my mum. My children were very fond of her and you could see the joy she got from them as well. They could tell which flat Granny lived in as there was a giant inflatable dolphin in the window! During this time, the whole family had occasional get-togethers when we attended the family picnic. We usually gathered at Peta's house and then went for a walk up on to the Malvern Hills. Sometimes we went up to The Wyche and towards Worcestershire Beacon or else to the Kettle Sings café on the next stretch of hills south of there. I often provided my well-known multi-coloured Victoria sponge which went down well although Bob's 'tomato eyes' are perhaps the best remembered event of those days. He put a small tomato behind each lens of his glasses to create bulging red eyes! They were the rare occasions when all the Lovering children, except David, of course, would meet up. The question of Mum's identity was raised at the picnics once or twice but, surprisingly, not much was said despite Mum herself never being present. Mum had problems with her feet and was unable to do much walking, so decided to stay at home instead.

Peta and Steve had a change in their lives as they had to leave the cottage in Stone Drive in Colwall. It was to be knocked down for a new housing development and Steve was due for retirement anyway. They found a flat in

Masefield Close in Ledbury which was only a few minutes away from Mum. This was perfect as it meant Mum and Peta were able to support each other. Mum often did some babysitting and Peta was always there to give Mum company when she needed it. They had much in common, including a lack of ability in dealing with their finances!

In 1997, Peta got the devastating news that she had an illness which might mean she only had a few months to live. The family tried to rally round and support her in any way that we could. I was glad that Mum lived so near to her in her time of greatest need. We then heard another piece of news, this time from Mum. Mike had contacted her and was going to visit her in Ledbury! He was now living in Scotland and had been looking after a disabled woman who had recently died. It was about sixteen years since he had contacted us and disappeared to Ireland. After his visit to Ledbury, he had suggested that Mum went to live with him in Scotland. Mum decided she would travel up and see whether she liked it up there. Within a few weeks of Mike reappearing, Mum had packed her bags, left the flat in Lawnside Road and gone to Kirriemuir, a small town, north of Dundee. Colin drove Mum up to Scotland. He told me that Mum showed him a photo of her and Mike that she had kept in her purse for the sixteen years he was missing. Mum said that she had never stopped loving Mike but I was really annoyed with her for deserting Peta when she needed Mum the most. She had left for a man who had suddenly disappeared, all those years before, without any explanation. My anger meant that, although I spoke to Mum occasionally on the phone, I would not see her again for a long time.

My children, Tom and Michael, went to Bristol Grammar School and, every other year, the school sent a group of pupils to the Edinburgh Fringe Festival to put on an improvisation show. Tom was keen to see his fellow pupils perform so we decided we would have a holiday up there. It was July 2005 and I had not seen Mum for nearly eight years. We were able to book a cottage in Corstorphine which was on the main road between Edinburgh Airport and the city. Whilst we were in Scotland, we decided we should visit Mum and Mike in Kirriemuir. This entailed catching a train, over the world famous Forth Railway Bridge, to Dundee. We then had a long bus ride to Kirriemuir, which was famed for being the home to the author, J.M. Barrie, creator of '*Peter Pan*'. Tom did not enjoy the long, winding journey on the bus, but it was good to be greeted by Mum and Mike when we finally arrived. We were shown to their house and it was quickly clear that Mike made a big fuss of Mum and did everything for her. I realised that I had misjudged Mike. Although I still felt it had not been good for Peta when he persuaded Mum to go to Scotland, it had undoubtedly been the right decision for Mum. For the first time in her life, she was not the one having to do all the hard work to keep a household functioning. She had someone else to do all the chores for her and to do the cooking. Given that Mum often burned the food when she cooked that was probably just as well. When we lived in Ledbury, chip pan fires were a regular occurrence when Mum was making tea, so no-one panicked when it happened. Mike had established himself in Kirriemuir as a clock and watch repairer and was highly regarded by the folk we met when Mike took us on a short tour of the town.

It had been good to see Mum looking so happy but the next time I visited her, things had completely changed. Mike died on 7th December later that year. I am not entirely sure of the cause, but it had a devastating effect on the mental health of Mum. Simon went up and helped to deal with the required paperwork and to arrange the funeral.

Amongst some of Mike's stuff, he came across a copy of his curriculum vitae which gave a little more detail of his life. His statement read: '

On leaving school in 1945, I served an apprenticeship in precision engineering until 1949, when I was called up for National Service with the Sappers. I later signed on as a regular soldier, serving in the Middle East & Far East theatres, finishing up as a plant & engine theory instructor at the SME at Chatham. I then worked for a while in Civil Engineering, which I always majored….' He then went into more detail of the jobs he had done before listing his hobbies: 'Nature conservation, hill-walking, Cacti and other succulents, crossword puzzles. I smoke a pipe; enjoy the friendship of my little dog- a Yorkie; I don't drink and my social activities are minimal.'

It was interesting that he mentioned that he did not drink. It seemed that he had finally conquered his demon. Another piece of paper was a reference on discharge from the Royal Engineers. It stated that he was discharged in

November 1959 because he was medically unfit. It went on to say "He is a very clean and intelligent man. He has a pleasant personality and will be a great asset to any employer".

I was not able to attend Mike's funeral but went up to Scotland a few weeks later. Mum was no longer in her home but had been admitted to Nine Wells Hospital in Dundee. As I walked down the corridor to her room, Mum passed me on a trolley, but she did not recognise me. The nurse informed me that Mum was going for a check-up and would be back in her room shortly. She explained that Mum was becoming a little incoherent and getting muddled, showing growing signs of dementia. I waited at Mum's bed. When she returned, Mum did realise it was me this time and thanked me for coming. She kept repeating "You know Mike is dead". It was clear she was still in a state of disbelief that she had lost the love of her life. The nurse had asked me to try to stimulate Mum as much as possible. It was tempting to try to get her to recall some incidents of her past, maybe describe where she came from! Instead of that, I found a crossword puzzle and started working on it with Mum's help. Mum had always been keen in doing all sorts of puzzles, but crosswords were her favourite. It was an enjoyable pastime which I had inherited from her too and we spent a good half hour mulling over some of the clues. It was reassuring to see that Mum's brain was still functioning even though she still drifted away at times and saying, "You know Mike is dead".

The following Summer, we made what was becoming an

annual trip to the Edinburgh festival and made the trek out to Kirriemuir. Mum was now staying in the Lisburn Nursing Home and she was certainly being well looked after. Mum's dementia had got a little worse and we were told that she often complained of aliens being in her room. She did not recognise me again, at first, and sometimes mistook me for Pauline! Tom and Michael enjoyed seeing Granny again even though it was a little disconcerting to see her in such a muddled state. She was not entirely on her own in her room; she had a small, but very heavy and solid, bust of Lenin on her bedside table. Of course, she also had her alien visitors to keep her company! We visited her in December as well and then during the next Edinburgh festival in the Summer and both her mental and physical health clearly declined over that period. On my last visit, just before Christmas in 2007, it was difficult to get much sense out of her. There were still a few glimpses of the old Mum, but she drifted off into another world every few minutes. At one point, one of the nurses entered the room where we were sitting. Mum suddenly asked, "Is that my father?". Sensing an opportunity, I replied, "I don't know. Shall I check? What is his name and I'll ask him?" Mum's mind had moved on to something else and she did not respond to my question. It was now over twenty-five years since Simon had told me about Mum and Dad and I had never directly asked who she really was. This was my last chance, but I did not take it. I think by then even Mum did not know who she was and, after being Marie Cremin for so long, she had probably erased her real identity from her memory entirely.

Not long after my visit, Colin and Simon drove Peta up

to Scotland so that she was also able to visit Mum. They had a similar experience as me. As they entered the home, they heard someone shouting "Dad!, Dad!". They remarked to the nurse that someone was having a bad time. The nurse replied, "That is your Mum!". They entered Mum's room and she thought Colin was her father and asked if she could sit by him. Colin held her hand, said "Hello", then asked if she had been to school. He then asked her what her name was and to spell it out! Mum said a name and began to spell it when Peta got upset and stopped Mum, saying "Don't worry about that now". The moment had gone and neither Simon nor Colin could work out what she had said. It sounded like Derricks or something similar. It might have been the last chance to hear her real name from Mum herself. Once again, Peta had intervened when Mum was about to tell us something.

Colin was able to visit Mum again on 20th February 2008. Mum was very weak with a serious chest infection. Before he left, Mum gave him a hug and rubbed his neck gently with her hand. Colin was deeply moved. It was the first time he could recall Mum showing such deep affection. As we had been growing up, Mum was always at work or sorting things in the home. There was little time for her to show her love for us in a physical way. Colin was about to start a new life living in Romania but, for Mum, it was the end. She died a few weeks later. ironically, she passed away on St Patrick's Day which was probably her way of getting back at her supposed Irish background. As with Dad's death, I felt a little detached from Mum when she died, so I did not grieve with any great emotion. I went to work in Yate as normal the following day. After work, I cycled to Nailsworth, about ten miles from Yate, to watch York City play at Forest Green Rovers. After the game finished, I had a late-night bike ride back to Bristol that took nearly two hours. I spent much of that journey thinking about Mum. Being alone, with my thoughts of her, was my way of coping with the loss. Once again, Simon took on the onerous task of travelling up to Scotland to sort out the funeral which was set to be on Monday, 31st March.

The day of the funeral was going to be a little awkward for me as Pauline and I had booked a wedding anniversary trip that weekend. We were going on a very romantic stay in Derry/Londonderry in Northern Ireland. We were due to return to Bristol Airport on Sunday evening, the day before the funeral. Pauline went home from the airport whilst I went through security again and waited for the flight to Edinburgh. I was staying in a Backpackers hostel near Waverley Station in Edinburgh and did not arrive until near midnight. It was over a pub-cum-disco and was quite noisy. I had to get up early in the morning to catch a train to Montrose where I would rendezvous with Simon. It felt quite weird to be in Montrose on a chilly, misty morning. It was a town I only knew through seeing the football results on *Grandstand*. It was only a short wait before Simon arrived. We then met up with Colin and I rode in the back seat of the car to the crematorium. I had my mp3 player and, naturally, listened to the song, '*In The Back Seat*' by The Arcade Fire. The song has the memorable line '*my family tree is losing all its leaves*'. This was to be the first funeral I had ever attended and we had just lost a huge branch in our family tree. The crematorium was in a wooded area in the middle of nowhere. The surreal morning continued when we got there and were met by Peta, Bob and Jan who had driven up from Herefordshire with Claudette. Apart from a few people from the nursing home, we were the only ones there. Simon read a fantastic eulogy which Mum would have liked. I am not sure she would have appreciated it if I had delivered the eulogy as I would have ended it by saying, 'she's dead'! I used to watch television with Mum when we lived in Ledbury and the comments ranged from 'Oh, doesn't he look old' when an old favourite appeared in a chat show to 'he's dead' when watching an old film. At the end of the service, we thanked the nursing staff for all they had done for Mum and headed to a pub in Kirriemuir to have a drink and share our memories of Mum. Having arrived from different parts of the country, we then dispersed to head home. Colin gave me a lift to Dundee and I got the train to Edinburgh, to fly home to Bristol. I was not alone on the flight- Lenin travelled home with me! It had been a very unusual day and although I had seen very little of Mum in the last ten years of her life, it was hard to believe she was no longer with us.

The family assembled again in July in Eastnor Park for the family picnic. For the first time, Mum came to this picnic as well or, at least, her ashes were there. The park seemed an appropriate place to scatter her ashes as we had spent a lot of time together as a family living in Eastnor before David and Peta got jobs and moved out. There is an oak tree by the small lake in the park, near to where we used to pitch our tents for camping holidays forty years before. We all took turns to spread her ashes around the base of the tree and say a few words. Mike's ashes were also scattered so Mum and Mike would be together forever. We got the cricket stuff out and had an enjoyable game before brewing some tea on the camp stove. We shared our stories of Mum once again. During the conversation, a solitary duck waddled up from the lake to join us. We joked that it was Mum re-incarnated as a duck coming to be part of the celebration of her life. It was actually quite a moving moment as we felt the spirit of Mum was present. The duck was not able to tell us what Mum's real name was. The only person who really knew the truth was Mum herself and she was now dead. Family research had become easier with the development of the internet and that might be our only hope now of getting to the bottom of the mystery. Mum did not have a gravestone, but we had a tree planted in the park with a plaque attached to commemorate Mum and Mike. Before we went our separate ways, we took the traditional group picture by the oak tree. Peta was still part of the group despite her big health scare ten years earlier when Mum had first gone to Scotland. We did not know it at the time, but it was to be the last time the five youngest children would be together.

6 SIMON

There had been a four-year gap after Peta's birth before the next of the Lovering children arrived. Simon Arthur Lovering was born on the British Army base in Moenchen-Gladbach, West Germany on 2nd October 1955. It was his birth being in Germany that had first led Mum to admit she and Dad were not married. Because of that age gap between the three eldest children and the rest of us, we three youngest children probably formed a stronger bond with each other. Colin and I both looked up to Simon. We probably experienced the toughest times as Dad was not around at all as we were growing up. Simon was always the most adventurous of the three of us whilst I was the one who always advised caution. Colin just did as he was told! In the garden of our Eastnor home, there were some lovely tall trees and Simon, naturally, wanted to climb as high as he could. I would climb the first few branches and then watch Simon continue higher and higher. "Watch out, Simon, that branch doesn't look too strong", I would warn, only to see him step on to it. We would often go for walks through Eastnor Park to the monument for the Somers family, which we could see from our house. Beyond that lay the Malvern Hills, stretching for many miles. Near one of the hills, Midsummer Hill, there was a quarry known as The Gullet. One day Simon and I were walking along the top of the cliff of the quarry and Simon decided he wanted to look over the edge. As he crouched to peer over, he lost his balance. I grabbed his arm and pulled him back. I do not think he fully appreciated the danger he had been in and he certainly did not thank me for saving his life. In fact, a few weeks later, we were playing a game where you had to throw a knife into the grass, near your opponent. Wherever the knife landed, the opponent had to move his foot to that spot. I think the game was called 'splits' and the first person to lose balance lost the game. Simon somehow managed, possibly deliberately, to stick the knife in my arm instead of the grass. It bled a lot and, although the damage was not too bad, I still have a scar on my arm to this day to remind me of the incident.

Although he was intelligent, the academic life was not for Simon. He did not pass his 11-plus exam so went to Ledbury County Secondary Modern School, the same school that Peta had just left. Simon particularly enjoyed his sport and at the end of his first year, he did a project on the Olympic Games. The Games were taking place in Mexico in 1968 and Simon used a roll of wallpaper backing paper to display the event. He collected newspaper cuttings which he stuck on to the paper. I was enthralled by it and helped him with the project. It certainly promoted my interest in all the Olympic sports and it earned Simon some House points at school. Those

Olympics were particularly memorable for Bob Beamon's enormous leap in the Long Jump and David Hemery's magnificent gold medal for Great Britain in the 400m Hurdles but it is the boxing that I recall most vividly. British boxer, Chris Finnegan, had reached his final and we decided to stay up to watch the fight. His fight was about the eighth tie on Finals night, which, being in Mexico, started after midnight. Simon dozed off during the second fight. I managed to stay awake through all the fights until just before Finnegan was due to step into the ring. I fell asleep and missed the fight. Somehow Simon had awoken just in time to see the bout and watch Finnegan claim the gold medal!

Simon's other favourite passion began around this time. Girls! When we went camping in Eastnor Park, he was always extra keen to come with us if there were Girl Guides camping there as well. Although in many ways, he was quite a shy person, he was always successful in his chatting up techniques. Being 'the most handsome of all the Lovering children' (his claim), this led to a succession of girlfriends in his life until he finally settled down and got married in his thirties. Simon joined the local Army Cadet Force in Ledbury and attended their meetings regularly. He would go on trips to the tank base in Bovington and camps at places such as Defford, near Worcester. On leaving school, aged fifteen, he decided that he would join the Army. He signed up for the Royal Engineers and left home for Dover in January 1972. Sadly, things did not work out and he left the Army after only six months. He returned home not really knowing what to do with himself. Simon got into a few bits of trouble before finding a job in Hereford working in a foundry at a factory. He also found himself a small flat by the rugby ground in Hereford. So began a life of working hard all week and then going to pubs and clubs at the weekend. I would occasionally go to Hereford and have an evening out with his friends. It was quite an education for me. Walking through the streets of Hereford they would regularly stop and look at themselves in the shop window reflections. Hair okay? Check. Clothes all right? Check Flies done up? Check. His friends called me 'The Bookworm' as I was successful at school but quickly realised that I knew as much about football and music as most of them. What I did not know was the latest dance craze. In one club, I was a little confused when everyone started sitting on the floor and began a rowing motion to The Gap Band's '*Oops Upside Your Head*'. Happy days. When the film '*Saturday Night Feve*r' came out in 1978, it was a lifestyle that I had witnessed to some degree in Hereford!

Hereford United were enjoying a huge period of success having recently been elected to the Football League. Simon became a keen fan and would travel to matches on most Saturdays and some midweek evenings. It was not, however, just to watch the football. It was the 1970s and football hooliganism in Britain was at its peak. Simon was a part of it. Walking through Hereford with him, he would point out locations where there had been a fight with Wrexham fans or whoever and tell me tales of trips to local rivals, Shrewsbury Town or Newport County. Living in the borders meant clashes with the Welsh clubs were particularly feisty occasions. I went to the odd

Hereford game, particularly as Simon's old school friend, Steve Emery, was now playing for the team as United got promoted up the League to the old Division Two. One season Hereford got drawn against my team, York City, in the Third Round of the FA Cup. I travelled up to York with Simon on the Hereford supporters' bus. York City won 2-1 and on the long return journey home I was sat with another Hereford fan, not Simon. I had to be careful not to reveal that I was a York City supporter. The draw for the next round was on the radio and I was the only person on the bus who was really interested in listening to it.

In between the occasional one-night stands, Simon did have some steady girlfriends and the one that probably had the biggest influence on him in those days was Vanessa. She was a teacher at a local secondary school and opened his eyes to a life beyond Hereford. She was the one who wanted to travel and that led to Simon needing a passport and finding out about Mum and Dad. Once he had made those first few trips abroad, he had the travel bug and wanted to discover more places. Being the adventurer, they were not always the usual tourist destinations. Vanessa decided that she wanted to take up a job in Turkey and Simon felt the loss of her companionship when she finally left England. A few years later, Simon himself nearly went to live abroad. He had fallen in love with a girl who was planning to work on a kibbutz in Israel and Simon decided to join her. We had a family party at Peta's house to say farewell to him but, as with his Army adventure, things did not work out and he once again returned home soon after.

On his return Simon set up home in another small flat in Worcester and got another job in a factory. He was now beginning to improve his management skills through being a Trade Union representative. Simon's love of travel continued, and he had a map in his flat on which he coloured the countries that he had visited. On one trip to the Far East, Colin was also in that part of the world and they agreed to meet up in Bangkok. Colin arrived first but Simon was delayed for some reason. Colin began to get quite concerned when there was no sign of Simon's flight. He was so relieved when Simon finally turned up that he gave him a big hug. Both were taken aback by the great show of affection they had towards each other and it certainly strengthened the bond between them. Over the years they would often travel together in far flung places around the globe.

Simon's other love, when he was not touring the world, was to go to theatrical shows, particularly musicals. He would occasionally visit us in Bristol to go to see a show, such as '*A Chorus Line*', and we would often sing the songs on the way home. One memorable evening was when we went to see '*A Man for All Seasons*' at the Theatre Royal in Bath. The production starred Charlton Heston and Simon was particularly keen to see one of the all-time Hollywood greats. Simon drove down from Worcester after work and we had a pre-show meal at a pizza restaurant next door to the theatre. Part way through the meal, Simon uttered the memorable phrase "The trouble with a pizza is that you get bored of eating it halfway through!". Whenever I have eaten pizza since I think of that comment. The show itself was very good, though I am not sure whether Simon enjoyed seeing the great actor. He fell asleep during the performance! Simon's favourite show was undoubtedly the musical '*Les Miserables*' which he saw several times.

Simon continued to enjoy nights out with his friends at the pubs and clubs in Hereford. On one of those nights, he met the love of his life, Karen Green, who was to become his wife in 1991. She also had a love of travel and they shared many adventures abroad as they both tried to visit as many countries as possible. Later, another big love also entered his life in the shape of a small terrier dog called Yogi.

With Mum's death, it seemed that our last chance of finding her real identity had gone but we felt that there may still be people alive who might know the truth. Research was made easier with the development of the internet. Tim, Bob's son, had already used the genealogical website, Ancestry UK, to find out about the Lovering family tree. I was given a subscription to the site for my birthday. I too could now do some Lovering hunting without having to travel down to London as I had done in the 1980s. I quickly found my way around the site and began compiling a Lovering family tree of my own. I was interested in tracing the Lovering family back through the generations as well as trying to solve the Mum mystery. Within a few minutes, I had all the details I had previously gained from those trips to London and they confirmed that there were no records of Dad and Marie Cremin having any children.

The next step, using Ancestry UK, was look for siblings

of Dad who may have married and had children. They would be my cousins and it made me realise that, apart from my sister and brothers and their children, I did not know any other direct relatives. My grandparents on Dad's side had died long before I was born and I did not know of any uncles and aunts that I might have, apart from godparents. Maybe with Ancestry UK, I would find new family members and I could also check whether any of those godparents were, in fact, blood relations. From our research at Catherine House, I knew that Dad had a brother Sidney George William Lovering who was two years older than him. I was able to see that he married Hilda Holmes in Barnes, London in 1933. Sadly, she died just four years later, and I could not find any children born to her. Sidney married again in September 1939 in Brentford, just at the outbreak of the Second World War, to Molly Bristoll. Sidney and Molly had two children: Barry, born in 1940, and Susan in 1943, both in Birmingham. Surely there was a good chance that Barry and Susan were alive and might know something about their Uncle Arthur running off with some woman after the War and abandoning his wife, Auntie Marie?

Ancestry was able to tell me that Susan had got married to Timothy Elliott in Somerset in 1962 and they had two children, Caroline and Nicholas. This was getting quite exciting, especially as I lived in Bristol. If they still resided in Somerset, that would be quite near to my home. As for Barry, the only record I could find suggested that he may have moved to the United States. I contacted my nephew, Tim, who had done all the research on the family tree, to ask about Barry and Sandra. To my surprise, he told me that he had been in contact with Barry a few years earlier. It seemed that Tim knew more than he had been telling us previously. He sent me a copy of the email he had received from Barry and said that Barry did not want to say much and that the correspondence ended there.

In the email, Barry said:

"...My dad was Sidney George William, Bill. My mum Molly Bristoll. I think they were married in 1939, I was born Dec 1940....My Sis, Sandra Jane or Batesy as she became known to everyone thanks to me; born Oct '43. My dad died after some sort of accident in 69. We hadn't seen him for years. Mum died in 74. My sister and I were estranged from everyone for years, including her kids. It was learned by chance that she died about 5 years ago but no-one knows under what circumstances."

I could not believe what I was reading. It appeared that Dad's brother's family had mysteries like our family. Barry's sister being estranged from her family bore similarities to David breaking off contact from us. He did not seem to know his father who left his family when Barry was young and then was unaware of how both his dad and sister died. I decided I would try to contact him again through email to see if he knew any more. He replied to my email. I sent him a photo of my Dad and asked if there were any similarities with his Dad but he said he could not remember what his Dad looked like! Tim had said that he did not want to say much but we exchanged a few messages. Although he could not tell me much, I gave him some details of his Uncle Arthur's family. He was able to tell me that his Dad had a job in

Birmingham, but then he and the family moved to a new job in Leicester. Sidney did not enjoy the new job and went back to his old job in Birmingham. The family continued to live in Leicester. Sidney would commute to work but then decided to live in Birmingham on his own and that was pretty much the last the family heard from him. Barry was now living in Florida and told me he was amazed when he walked into a local bank and the teller was called Chester Lovering. Barry had also received an invitation to join the Lovering Family Society. He declined the offer.

Further research on Ancestry also revealed that Dad did, in fact, have two more older brothers: Leonard, born in 1906, and Herbert, born in 1907. Leonard had married twice and had one son, also called Barry, born in 1944. I wondered where those elder brothers were living now. It turned out that both had emigrated to Canada to add to the large number of Loverings in North America. I would try to find out more about them but first I wanted to see if I could discover any more about Sidney, or Uncle Bill as I should call him, and his daughter Sandra. I tried to Google his name using the search engine on the computer. Rather surprisingly, it came up with some results that led me to The National Archive. There were references to two documents concerning Sidney, but neither were available for public viewing due to an order stating they were not to be released for a further seventy years. This was a curious turn of events and quite intriguing. What on Earth had he done to merit the files being closed for so long? Perhaps he was a spy too, just as we had hypothesised that maybe Mum had worked for the Germans during the War!

I made a Freedom of Information request to The National Archive asking why the files were not to be available to the public for such a long time. A few weeks later I got a response. It had been decided that the files could become available for inspection but with parts redacted. The reason given was that it could upset living members of his close family. Even more intriguing! It was a few months before the documents were made available, so I was then able to plan my visit to inspect them.

Some of the files held at The National Archive are accessible online but those relating to Sidney were not, so I had to make the journey to Kew in London to see them. I had organised my reader's card and booked to have the files available for collection on my arrival. Only pencils, not pens, were allowed in the Readers' Room and I was searched before entering. I was allowed to take my iPad in with me and I could use that to photograph any documents. I collected a document wallet and sat down at my designated table to sieve through the various letters and papers in the wallet. It was quite staggering to think that these documents had been kept; some of them typed up with mistakes, some with little hand-written comments. As I worked my way through them, I became more and more aware of the very sad last few years of Sidney's life. Once or twice, I would stop and say, 'Oh, no', to myself. I felt great pity for Sidney as I read more of the documents.

He split from Molly in July 1954 and a document refers to divorce proceedings in February 1959. The early letters referred to a debt that Sidney owed to the taxman. Another letter about the debt then revealed what Sidney was going through:

'You acknowledged our letter and were good enough to advise us of Mr Lovering's mental illness'.

This was followed by another document relating to a maintenance payment to Molly and other costs. They kept referring to the patient and it became clear that Sidney had been admitted into the Rubery Mental Hospital in Birmingham. Sidney was being asked to pay for the upkeep of his wife and two children as the divorce went through the courts though it emerged that Molly did not want to make the decree nisi absolute because she might suffer hardship. She had been badly treated by her husband prior his being retained in hospital.

The details of his condition were stated by a solicitor:

'The patient was admitted here on 8.2.1960 with a diagnosis of Korsakov's Psychosis... he is totally disorientated in time and place and unable to give a proper account of himself, and is euphoric. He is obviously suffering from a severe degree of dementia'.

A visitors' report in 1964 notes:

'Patient showing mental deterioration and is incapable of any but the simplest of tasks. His health is good but requires constant supervision to keep him clean. Watches TV. No contact with family. Wears hospital clothing'

Eight months later, the same visitor reports:

'There is a marked deterioration inpatient's mental condition. He has much vomiting and bladder trouble. Is very unsteady on his feet. He speaks with difficulty and is hard to understand. A friend Mr Page pays a very short visit every quarter'.

A year later:

'No visitors. Goes to cinema and watches TV'.

Still no visitors reported another year later.

Sidney died intestate at Hollymoor Hospital on 24th June 1968 and Molly became entitled to the whole of his estate amounting to about £1000. His funeral took place in July 1968 at Lodge Hill Crematorium and there is a letter from the funeral arrangers, a year later, demanding the fee for costs of the funeral. Even in death, Sidney's troubles were not over. I felt quite depressed when I left the The National Archive and went to have lunch in a nearby café to mull over the sadness of my Uncle Bill's final years.

I wrote to Barry again to tell him of my findings. He responded:

'I did not know the details. My mother received notice of his death and we attended his funeral. Can't remember where. I think we were the only ones present. Pretty dismal'.

He later wrote:

'I have no idea where the church was or where he is buried. As you know he left us when I was 14 or so and we had little or nothing to do with him afterward and did not mind at all, except that it left our Mum in a bind. She bought a Knitmaster to make sweaters for sale. She became secretary to (I think) the chancellor of Leicester University. Their office was a mansion which had belonged to the Attenborough family. Yes those Attenboroughs. Eventually she moved to London as well'.

I also asked if Barry knew anything at all about his father's brothers.

'No, I've never heard of them. As kids we knew nothing of our parents' details. Growing up we spent a lot of time with my mother's family, cousins, hols, etc and our dad was never involved. Don't recall ever meeting any of his family or hearing anything about them. I don't know why. Mum's family were great and we loved being with them. I don't know what Dad's problem was. Weird'.

His story sounded so familiar as I knew nothing of Dad's family either. Only problem was, I also knew nothing of Mum's background.

My research into Mum continued. I used the Google search engine again to see if there was a convent school in Louvain in Belgium. Mum had told stories about her life there, but did it still exist? I got a result, which included a contact email address. I decided to send an enquiry. I asked if there was anyone called Helen, who probably came from London, who might have attended. I did not expect to be successful in this quest but, rather amazingly, I got a reply the next day.

The email read:

'We do have a record of the pupils but I don't find anybody named Helen between 1930 and 1940. However, I did find a Helen Godfrey (but it is not put from where she came) who arrived here as a boarder on 5th October 1926 and left on 23rd July 1927. The only one coming from London in the 1930s is a certain Pamela Lees who arrived here in 1932. In 1936 there is a Helen van der Goes who came from Holland. I don't know if this can help you and I am sorry to be able to find more.'

I thanked them for their help and then thought about the names given. Helen Godfrey would seem to be too old to be Mum, but Mum could well have been born earlier than we thought. I cross referenced with my list of Cambridge Blues and there was no Godfrey, nor indeed, a van der Goes. Being from Holland would not be a total surprise given Mum told us of being in Germany when she was young.

The internet was proving useful, which was great whilst it was working. In early 2011, we were having trouble with our telephone connection. The landline (provided by BT) was dead which meant we had no access to the internet either (also BT). When the line was restored, there was a message on Facebook for my son, Michael, from Simon saying, 'Get your Dad to contact me'. I phoned Simon to be told the stunning news that Bob had died the previous night from a massive heart attack. Bob had been in hospital before Christmas to have some polyps removed. The operation had been successful, and Bob was at home recuperating. He was about to go to bed on the evening of 12th February when he had the heart attack and passed away quite quickly. I was relieved that it seemed that he did not suffer a long death but was completely stunned to have lost one of my brothers. I was in a state of shock and found it difficult to comprehend that Bob was no longer with us and there would be no humorous words of wisdom and amusing stories. The family tree had lost another leaf.

The funeral took place at the crematorium in Hereford on Friday 25th February. Pauline drove us up the beautiful Wye Valley and we met the rest of the family at the Memorial pub, not far from the crematorium. We stood around waiting and it was only when the coffin finally arrived that it really hit home that Bob had gone. Many people broke down in tears as the coffin was carried into the chapel which was packed with friends and family. It was testament to Bob's popularity that so many had made the effort to come and say farewell to him. He had impacted on the lives of all sorts of people through the jobs at the bookies, in the clothes shop and in his last job at Sun Valley in Hereford. Simon, once again, did a magnificent job in presenting a eulogy to Bob which brought more tears, both of sadness and of joy, of what Bob had given us. The family continued to reminisce about his life when we gathered afterwards at his house with Jan, his widow. Later we went to The Barrels pub in the middle of Hereford which Bob frequented throughout his life. Among the mourners that gathered there were some members of Mott the Hoople, and other musicians. Music played a huge part in his life, and I had got to know some bands through Bob, such as Stackridge. Bob had also raved about a new band called The Decemberists and I bought their album less than a month before Bob died. The title? '*The King Is Dead*'. How very appropriate.

That evening, we travelled to Worcester to have a meal together. It was good for the three youngest brothers to be together, along with some their children. Bob's death probably brought us closer together though we remarked that it was rather sad that the family only got together at big events. We agreed that we should make more of an effort to keep in touch with each other. Using Facebook could help with that. Even many years after his death, Bob's Facebook page was still open with his last entry on 3rd January 2011 reading: 'Off for my op. in the early morning...call Jan in the evenings for any updates..in the meantime love to you all for the New Year.....'

I liked to think that we were still in contact with him, so I checked his Facebook page regularly for the next update from him. Nothing, so far!

I had lost one brother which made me even more determined to regain another, David. He needed to know that not only had Mum died but now his closest brother had also gone. This time I hoped the search for him might be easier as we had the power of the internet to help. I found a site which helped you to search for missing family or friends, so I submitted David's name. Back came two or three possibilities but, given we last knew David was living in Canterbury, I went for the one living in Kent. I paid for the details of the address and then wrote a letter, enclosing a stamped addressed envelope for a reply. In the letter I said that I might be his brother and gave him my details. I also asked for a reply whatever the outcome and said that if he was my brother but wanted no contact with the family then please reply anyway and I would respect his wishes. It was my birthday a week later. Amongst the birthday cards was the stamped addressed envelope I had sent. It had been returned from Kent and I opened it eagerly. To my joy, it was from my brother. David seemed quite pleased to have received my letter and included his telephone number. This was one of the best birthday presents that I had ever received. I immediately got on the phone to call him. It was good to hear his voice again. I told him the news of Mum and Bob which saddened him greatly. He then explained that the reason that he had cut himself off from the family. It was because Mum was constantly asking him for money right from the time he started work at The Feathers in Ledbury. His patience ran out and it was very difficult for him to say no to her requests. He had decided that the best thing to do was to have no contact at all with her or the rest of the family. This confirmed that my theory that maybe David was not really Mum's child was not true, though we realised that when we saw the resemblance between Mum and him when we had last visited him.

I wrote another letter to David including various family photos and bringing him up to date with what else had happened in the family. I also broke the news to him about Mum and Dad having never been married which surprised him greatly. He began to phone me regularly which was good although the chat mainly consisted of sport, music and how good his new iPhone was. I also became aware of how wonderful Poundland shops are and the fact that there are three of them in Ashford where he lived. I was determined to visit him and arranged to travel to Ashford near to his birthday in May. In our conversations, he had mentioned that he seen The Rolling Stones in *The Rock 'n' Roll Circus* in the late 1960s. I therefore bought him a DVD of that event to give to him for his birthday. I hoped that he might appear in the film, but it turned out that he could not be seen in any of the scenes.

The journey to Ashford International was quite exciting as I travelled on a new Javelin train which raced through the Kent countryside on the railway track constructed for Eurostar. It was a smooth, fast journey and I soon arrived in Ashford. I found my way to David's flat in Canterbury Road which looked quite run down from the outside. I knocked on the door and, after a short wait, the door opened. I was greeted by David. He had not changed that much since the last time I saw him though he was, of course, much older. He walked with the aid of a stick and he was on medication for his ailing limbs. In his front room were hundreds of DVDs and CDs and one of the first things he did was to show me all the channels he could get on his new television. He was now retired from working in the record shop, but his walls were adorned with photos of various pop stars he had met. It was frustrating for me to have missed his time working in the record trade given how important music had been to me all my life. It was interesting to hear his stories about the family. He remembered that when the family went camping in Germany, Mum would stay at home, but a woman called Barbara went with them. It may have been completely innocent, but David suspected that she might have been Dad's mistress! He also claimed that another mistress of Dad was a well-known actress that he met in the early 60s. David had last seen Dad when he met him at a service station around the time of Peta's wedding in 1968. I did not stay too long, but I was glad to have made a physical re-connection with David. It felt like I had gained a brother. This time I would ensure that we did not lose contact with him again!

The next time I visited him, David showed me a document that had been produced by a friend of his. He had asked him to do some research into the family history to see if he could discover any more than we had found out already. The document made interesting reading and it was clear that David had made contributions to it, as well, by providing a little inside knowledge, though it was quite vague in places. On the electoral register for one year when Mum and Dad were living at De Vere Gardens in Kensington, Mum was listed as Marie H. Lovering – another confirmation that her real name is almost certainly Helen. It said Dad was posted to Rheindahlen from 1952 until 1960 but omitted to mention that he must also have been in Strensall, near York, in 1957 when I was born. David confirmed his story about the woman accompanying the family on camping trips adding that he thought she was a school teacher called Barbara Luke who had her own car.

Another entry said: 'posted to Cyprus circa 1960/62. HM Army Colonel. It was said that the family could not go to Cyprus with him as he was only going for six months though it later transpired that his relationship with

Helen was long since over. He remained in Cyprus for two years'.

In 1965- 'Married Claire A. E. Foster in Westminster Jun 1965. (could have been a bigamous marriage as he may have still been married to Marie Cremin'.

1966- 'Opened the Wimpy Bar (Manager) in Nottingham, England'.

I asked David about this as it seemed quite strange that Dad left the Army to work in a Wimpy bar only to later get a job with the Ministry of Defence. It was something that had always puzzled me. David was not sure of the circumstances but had heard a story that the Wimpy restaurant was part of the cinema building. When The Beatles played there, they set up a false fire alarm to distract the fans waiting outside so the band members could leave the venue relatively easily without being mobbed. David's document also stated that, around this time, Dad appears to have broken off any contact with Helen and the children, although I know, from my diary entries, that he did still occasionally send money to Mum. Nothing new arose from the exercise but it showed that David was keener to find out the truth about Mum than Bob had been willing to show.

Soon after, I arranged another trip to Ashford for Peta so that she could visit her brother too. I booked her train ticket from Ledbury and met her at Paddington Station. We got the tube to St Pancras Station where we met up with my eldest son, Tom. Tom was staying in London and wanted to meet his long-lost uncle David. Tom had, unfortunately booked his ticket for Ashford in Surrey rather than Ashford International but he was able to get a refund! Peta had brought an empty suitcase with her as David had promised to give Peta's grand-daughter, Izzy, lots of freebies he had got from newspapers, including Lego pieces and some DVDs. I was pleased that David had met more members of the family. I hoped that he might be able to come to stay in Bristol but that was going to be difficult as he was not physically very mobile. It would also be quite an overwhelming experience to meet lots of members of the family all at once. Neither Colin nor Simon seemed particularly interested in meeting him again. Simon was quite forthright in saying he did not want to talk to him. I can understand his opinion that it was David who had decided to abandon the family, but I sensed that David really wanted to re-connect again. We had recently lost Bob and I hoped that would have increased the importance of family connections. Nevertheless, I could not persuade Simon to contact David.

When Simon and Bob both worked in Hereford, I would regularly visit them. We would sometimes spend the lunchbreak going round the putting greens by the River Wye opposite Hereford Cathedral. Simon later took his golf a little more seriously and played on proper courses round the world. I joined Simon for an evening out in Hereford one Friday. The following morning, Simon suggested that we went to Belmont Golf Club as he fancied a practice round. What I didn't know was that the journey to the course would involve crossing the River Wye or, more precisely, wading across the River Wye!

Simon had prepared for this by wearing short trousers. I had not. I was wearing jeans and had to roll them up my legs and do my best to keep them dry- unsuccessfully as it turned out. Years later, when he had settled into his home with Karen in Worcester, Simon became a member of The Gaudet Luce Golf Club in Droitwich where he gained much respect amongst the members. He was even elected the Club Captain one year. Many of his travels abroad often involved finding a local golf course and trying it out. He was pleased that Mum had settled in Scotland where there was no shortage of courses to challenge him. Colin had also got the golf bug and would join Simon on the fairways whenever the chance arose. This was not always for the good of the family as there was an occasion when my eldest son, Tom, was home from the United States for a few weeks. We arranged a family get together at The Prince of Wales in Ledbury. I was unable to attend due a prior arrangement to attend a conference. Colin had flown over from Romania but neither he nor Simon appeared at The Prince. It transpired that they had both spent the afternoon on the golf course. Getting the Lovering family together was never an easy task!

Simon's career took a different direction as he had moved off the shop floor of factory work and became an educator instead. He was now training adults in various aspects of vocational work and qualifications. I was quite proud of his progress given how his own schooling had gone. At last, he was able to use his personal skills and knowledge to help other people. I was quite amused that, when he was teaching a Number qualification, he sent me the homework question he was going to set his students and asked me for the answers. I was a teacher myself and recognised the importance of being at least one step ahead of your students!

A memorable travel adventure for Simon and Karen was when they flew to New York and returned across the Atlantic Ocean in the luxury cruise liner, the Queen Mary 2. Poor communication between the members of the Lovering family was again highlighted by the trip. Pauline, Michael (our youngest son) and I were visiting Tom in Boston, USA where he was studying for a PhD at Harvard University. Whilst in Boston, we were going to travel by bus to New York to stay overnight in a hotel on 42nd Street. Through messaging on Facebook, we discovered that Simon and Karen were due to set sail the day before we were due to arrive. We had no idea that they had gone to New York. It would have been great to wave them off on their journey home. Michael and I visited the Intrepid Air and Space Museum which was adjacent to the quayside that the Queen Mary 2 had sailed from the day before. On our return flight home from Boston, we did at some point fly over the ship. It was on this trip that Simon and Karen got to know the British Olympic 400m runner Derek Redmond and they became quite good friends. Derek Redmond is remembered for pulling his hamstring at the 1992 Barcelona Olympics and being helped across the finishing line by his father. He was disqualified because he had been given assistance but went into athletics folklore.

Another example of the Lovering family organisation, or

rather the lack of it, was when we agreed to meet up at Winter Wonderland in Hyde Park, London, on a chilly Saturday in December. I caught the train to Paddington and, after having something to eat, walked across the park to Wonderland. I tried to contact the others and Matt, Colin's youngest son, said they were on the way. Shortly after, I was told that they had decided it was too far to walk to Wonderland and had decided to go to a pub near Paddington Station instead. I duly walked back across the park to the pub. When I got there, we heard that Dan, Colin's eldest, and his wife, Stacey had gone to Wonderland as well, only to be told of the change of plans. Fortunately, Simon and Karen had gone back to their hotel to have a rest and found out about the pub rendezvous before they made the fruitless trip to Wonderland also!

Simon and Karen also followed in Bob's footsteps and paid a visit to Malta. Dad had died about thirty years before, but Simon was keen to find where he had been laid to rest, at sea. On the last day of their holiday, they went to where birth, marriage and death records for Malta are kept and were able to obtain a copy of Dad's death certificate. It gave details of the cause of death: congestive heart failure, mitral incompetence and mitral valve replacement, plus pulmonary oedema. It also stated that he was 'buried at sea 45 degrees off Dragonara Point 5 meteres(sic) off in a depth of 100m'. Five metres off seemed a little close to the land so I suspect it should have read five miles instead. I looked up burials at sea on the internet. It was amusing to read of burials that went wrong including one where the coffin was not given sufficient weight and floated back to the surface! To make matters worse, the lid had come off the coffin to expose the dead body within. I hoped that Dad's funeral went without any mishap. Another thing of note on the death certificate was that Dad's parents were recorded too. His mother's maiden name is given as Smith rather than Grindlay. It appeared that, just like us, Dad did not know the name of his mother either!

On their return home, Simon described the events of their stay in Malta. He said that they made their way to Dragonara Point, which lies a few miles north-west of the capital, Valletta. They took a small bunch of flowers which they threw into the sea- 5 metres off the coast- and said a few words. I was pleased that, at last, one of Dad's children was able to see his final resting place and show some respect. There was also a tinge of sadness that he had cut himself off from his six children and that some of us never really knew him. Simon also mentioned that there seemed a possibility that his widow was still alive, but he and Karen were due to return home the following day and were not able to do more research. If she was still alive, perhaps she might be able to shed some light on Mum or Marie Cremin.

7 RICK

This chapter could be called Ricky as that is what the family called me when I was young, and some still do. I dropped the 'y' when I was about twelve years old as I thought it sounded a little babyish. The only time I identified with 'Ricky' was when watching a television series, *'Champion, The Wonder Horse'* as the young boy in that was also called Ricky. I also liked the Steely Dan song *'Rikki Don't Lose That Number'*. The teachers at secondary school called me Richard so you could tell what people were to me by what they called me. Ricky meant family, Richard meant teacher, Rick meant friend and anything else meant they did not like me! I once made the mistake of saying that I hated the name Dick.

I was born on 6th November 1957 in the Maternity Hospital in Fulford, York. Until very recently, whilst writing this book, I thought I had been born at the Military Hospital which used to be opposite Imphal Barracks, in Fulford. Through discussions on the York Past and

Present Facebook page, I discovered there had also been a Maternity Hospital, two miles down the road and my birth certificate confirmed that is the most likely place of birth. It seemed ironic that I had been doing research to find out who Mum was and where she was born, and all along, I had my own birthplace wrong! Sadly, my birthplace no longer exists. It was pulled down to make way for a designer label shopping outlet so there is nowhere to hang the blue plaque!

I was christened Richard James Lovering. I have no idea why my parents chose that name, but I now think at least one of the children might have been named after Mum's father. I like my name and, when a kid, used to enjoy the fact that I shared my name with many Kings of England (even more if you count Kings of Scotland!). I also like the fact that I was born in England as I could so easily have been born in Germany like Simon and my younger brother, Colin. I do not know the reason why Dad had a break from being stationed in Germany and spent some time at Strensall, north of York instead, but that posting has greatly affected my life. On the plus side, it led to me attending the University of York where I met my wife, Pauline. The downside was that I became a lifelong supporter of York City football club. York City provided a few seasons of joy but, generally, it meant I had to put up with a lot of stick from friends following the all too frequent poor displays. Of the six children, I am probably the only one who has followed a conventional path through life: school, university, two steady teaching jobs then retirement. I was fortunate that Mum valued my education so much that I was allowed to stay at both

Eastnor Primary School and Ledbury Grammar School when the family moved elsewhere.

I was the first pupil to pass the 11-Plus exam at Eastnor Primary for several years, so I knew absolutely no-one when I started at Ledbury Grammar School in September 1969. We had been living in Ledbury for several months before I left Eastnor School and I had caught the bus to school each day. I knew many of Simon's friends in Ledbury who would refer to me as 'Simon's brother'. After being at the Grammar School for a while, I felt real satisfaction at Simon now being referred to as 'Rick's brother' by my friends. It may seem a small thing to many people but going to the Grammar School is where I first felt a little more independent from the rest of the family. I was successful academically and I certainly saw that success as a path forward for me. I was determined that I was going to be self-sufficient when I grew up and not have to lead the financially poor life I had suffered as a child. Despite that self-confidence in my ability, I was quite surprised to find that I came top in the end of First year exams which meant I received a prize on Speech Day. It was a feat that I was to repeat in both the Second and Third years too, winning more prizes. I lost my crown in the Fourth form when I came a narrow second to a new pupil in the school, John Istance. There were no prizes for coming second in the Fourth Year. In the first three years, both first and second were able to choose a book as a prize to be awarded on Speech Day. That fall from top spot was partly due to me wanting to take up a new challenge. I wanted to improve my performances on the sports field.

I had always enjoyed watching sports and playing football, but I wanted to see if I could achieve more success. I started to think more carefully about what I ate and did much more exercise. I was an average footballer though I did have a reputation for scoring goals. I was pleased to have a record of scoring a goal for every team I ever played for, even including one off games for school staff teams against pupils and for the university team despite that I only played a few times. Rugby was played at the Grammar School and, because there were only twenty-one boys in my year, it was not difficult to get into a team of fifteen. We lost every game, bar one, until we played Lucton School at the start of the Third Year and won 95-0! I scored my first try which I would like to describe as a mazy run from the halfway line beating several defenders along the way. Unfortunately, the truth was that their fullback had the ball in his in-goal area and passed the ball to me. I caught it and gratefully touched it down! At half-time, our PE teacher came over to give the team talk. He had been concentrating on another game on a neighbouring pitch and so did not know the score. He was a little furious and wanted to know why we were kicking so many penalties towards the goal. We informed him that they were conversions and that we were winning 55-0. The second half was shortened to ease the pain of our poor opposition. The following Monday the results were announced by the deputy head in assembly: 'The Under 14s have won…..(he turned to other staff)..are you sure this is correct?...(staff nodded)… The Under 14s beat Lucton 95-0'.

The school 1st XV team was selected from years Five

and Six so it was harder for me to nail down a place in the side. By now I was playing in the backs. I think I must have reached my final adult height by the time I was about fourteen years old as this is reflected in my playing positions. I started playing as a Lock Forward in the second row in the First Year then moved to the back row and ended up on the Wing by the time that I left school. I was very disappointed when I was not selected for the team one week. In the end, I did play as someone dropped out and I scored a try which was very satisfying. I started writing reports of the 1st XV fixtures for the local newspaper, The Ledbury Reporter. I tried, where possible, to include some mention of me. It is always good to see your name in print. I stretched that desire for recognition a little when I wrote that 'Richard Lovering missed the conversion and the match finished 20-14'. My crowning glory in sport at school is when I beat two of the star athletes in the 400m on Sports Day and in the District Championship. I went to the County Championships and came sixth in the Final. When I was in the Sixth Form, I frequently helped with sports with the younger pupils, particularly with athletics in the Summer months. I am certain that it was this experience which finally convinced me that I wanted to be a teacher. My only regret is that I do not think any of my family ever came to watch me play rugby or anything. That was probably just as well as, many years later, Pauline brought baby Tom to watch me play cricket for the Staff team against Chipping Sodbury School. They arrived a little late. I had opened our innings and, by the time they got there, I was already out. What was worse, I had scored my first ever duck!

I had great success in the classroom and had also achieved a great deal in my sporting endeavours. The same could not be said for my love life. I was already eighteen years old before I got my first steady girlfriend.

It was the long hot, dry Summer of 1976 and I had just completed my 'A' levels and left school. I was about to start a job at the local jam factory, Ledbury Preserves, whilst I awaited my results to see if I got a place at university. I would occasionally babysit for Peta and Steve on a Saturday evening. I stayed at their home in Colwall overnight and then walked up on the Malvern Hills the following day. One Sunday afternoon, I decided to walk to the lake at Earnslaw as it was a hot, sunny day. I took my shoes and socks off, sat on a rock, and dipped my feet in the refreshingly cold water. The lake was not very busy, despite the heat, and my attention was drawn towards three girls who were messing about on the lake in a small dinghy. I watched them for about half an hour before realising that I had also gained their attention. They were coming off the water and heading towards me. We had a drink of water and began a conversation. I discovered that they were called Ann, Becky and Carol, all aged fifteen, and went to Malvern Girls' College. We talked for nearly two hours and they mentioned that one of their friends was having a party. They asked whether I would like to come. Of course, I said I would like to go to the party and I gave them my contact details. It was getting late and they had to go home so we said our farewells. It had been an enjoyable afternoon and I looked forward to hearing from them again. The only downside to the day was that, when I got home, Mum told me that the budgie had disappeared!

I started work at the jam factory the following week. Working in a factory could be a monotonous experience and the hot weather made the days unbearably long. It made me appreciate, a little, the sort of life that Simon had led in his working life. You spend the entire week looking forward to the weekend when you could be released from the shackles of boredom. Each day, I would go home and hope that a letter would be awaiting me from the three Malvern girls. Weeks passed and still nothing arrived. At the factory, I was now working on the jam line with a fellow student, David Mapp, who was a couple of years younger than me. He made life at work more bearable as we spent the day stacking jars of jam on to a pallet whilst telling each other amusing stories. There were two production lines in our section. We were on the manual line. The other was more automated and, consequently, more pallets of jam were produced on that line. Dave and I decided we would try to improve the efficiency of our stacking to try to match the production on our line with that on the automated line. One example of this was that normally, when a pallet was full, one of us would find the forklift driver and ask him to collect the pallet. The ladies on the line liked this as it was a chance for a break as the line would halt whilst we waited for the driver to arrive. We knew we could speed things up by one of us going for the driver before the pallet was completed. The other would continue to stack so the driver was ready just as the pallet was full. We were not popular with the ladies as it meant no break, but we achieved our aim. One day, production on our line exceeded that of the automated line. Our challenge had made life at work almost enjoyable and there was further joy for me. I received a letter from one of the girls inviting me to a party in Malvern. It was from Carol, and she had even arranged a lift for me from the Market House in Ledbury.

The day of the party arrived. I had been to Bob's shop in Hereford to buy some new shirts and I also wore my blue velvet jacket. I spent the evening chatting to Carol and getting to know her. She was a really interesting person. I knew I wanted to go out with her but did not have the courage to make a move during the party. The evening ended and we were back in the car to take me home. I was in danger of missing this opportunity, so I suddenly asked Carol if she fancied a walk on the hills the following afternoon. She said 'yes' and, as we happened to be passing through the centre on Great Malvern, I said, 'Okay, I'll meet you outside W.H.Smiths at 2pm'! I stayed in Colwall overnight and then walked back to Malvern again after lunch. I met Carol as arranged and we went for a walk to St Anne's Well and to Worcestershire Beacon. This time I felt much more comfortable with her. We exchanged our first kisses before I walked her home again. As I noted in my diary that night, it had certainly been a very good day as I even got a free train journey back to Ledbury! The following Sunday, Carol invited me back to her home to meet her parents and have tea. Her parents lived in a very nice semi-detached house and they were very kind to me. It would be a while before I had the courage to introduce Carol to my family and take her back to the second floor flat in Ledbury where we lived but I now had very first proper girlfriend.

I received my exam results a few weeks later which confirmed that I had got a place at the University of York to study Mathematics with Education. I made the most of my time with Carol before, in October, I set off on the train for York. It seemed a little unfair that I now had a girlfriend but had to leave her and go so far away. I returned home a couple of times each term but, otherwise, the only time we had together was during the vacations. We talked on the phone every Sunday, appropriately at 2pm, and regularly wrote letters to each other. This was long before texts and emails were invented!

Carol was three years younger than me and, with the long periods without seeing each other, it was inevitable that there would be a strain on the relationship. We went out together for two years, but I knew Carol was getting restless. When we finally did part, I found it very difficult. It was an amicable split and Carol was very supportive of me. We even spent the following New Year's Eve together. We kept in touch even when she went to university in Exeter and went on various trips abroad to Sicily and Zurich but, eventually lost contact as both our lives moved on. Fast forward to the early 2000s and I am at home in Bristol after a long day at work. I was reading the Bristol Post with the television on and a Party Political Broadcast on behalf of the Green Party comes on. I was half watching it whilst reading the paper and suddenly glimpsed someone who looked very familiar. I was sure that it was Carol! I watched keenly to see her again, but she did not appear again in the broadcast. I grabbed the Radio Times to see if it would be shown again later that evening. I was in luck, and I was able to view it once more. It was indeed Carol, only now she called herself Caroline, and she was a councillor in Oxfordshire. In later years, she would become the leader of the Green Party and be elected to the European Parliament. In the General Election of 2010, Caroline Lucas became the first ever Green Party candidate to win a seat in Parliament. A couple of years later, she was giving a talk in Bristol, so I contacted her to arrange to have a cup of tea together. We chatted for about half an hour. Although it was now over thirty years since we split, it seemed like it had been only the week before, as we talked about what we had done with our lives. I was so inspired by her talk that evening that I decided to join the Green Party myself. I had always been interested in politics and complaining about this, that and the other, so I felt it was time to become actively involved. Simon was dismayed as he told me I had joined the wrong party. He was a trade unionist and staunch Labour Party supporter.

After the split with Carol, I was not ready to have another relationship and was not much fun to be with at times for a year. I completed my degree and decided to stay on at York for a further year to train to be a teacher and obtain the PGCE qualification. I got my name in the Ledbury Reporter again, this time on the front page, with the small headline: 'Honours degree for Richard'. Ledbury was such an excting place to live. Back in York, I was now a graduate so was able to have a larger room to live in. I was still residing in Derwent College which was very appropriate as I was born in the district of Derwent in York. I went to the Freshers' Ball where my attention was drawn to three girls (again!). I got talking to them and invited them back to my room for a cup of tea or coffee. All three girls were studying mathematics and their names were Janet, Jenny and Karen but I was attracted to Janet, the girl from Manchester. There was a party the following evening and I saw Janet dancing with another guy. When I got the chance, I moved in and got talking to Janet and we spent the rest of the evening together. I had found a new girlfriend and this time she lived just down the stairs and along the corridor, rather than at the other end of the country. There was only one problem: she already had a boyfriend back in Manchester. I was starting my teaching practice which meant getting up early in the morning. It was quite frustrating that I could no longer lead the life of a student, staying up to the early hours, putting the world to right. Janet and I saw a lot of each other and everything was good until she told me that her boyfriend was coming to York to visit her. That cooled the relationship somewhat and the Saturday that he came to York was hard to bear. I tried to keep out of the way and was grateful for the moral support of my friends who recognised the turmoil I was suffering. The following morning, there was a knock on my door. It was Janet and she was looking very upset. She informed me that she had split up from her boyfriend. I did my best to console her whilst inside my heart was jumping for joy.

It was hard work being on teaching practice, but I was able to come 'home' to college to Janet each evening. It meant that my final year in York was a happy one. I applied unsuccessfully for a couple of jobs in York before getting the phone call from my old school in Ledbury offering me a job. I accepted the job which would mean that, once again, I would be living away from my girlfriend – the reverse of the locations with Carol! I knew that situation would be difficult for the both of us. That summer, I visited Janet at her home in Irlam, Manchester. We went to see the film, '*Gone With The Wind*' with both of us realising that we needed to discuss our future. The film seemed never ending, unlike our relationship which had to give. I had expected the worse, but it was still hard to leave Janet. I caught the train home to Ledbury the following morning. We could have tried to make it work but I feared that I might be the 'boyfriend at home' who would be dumped when Janet met someone else. I still had friends in York, and wanted to watch York City play, so I returned there during the first half-term holiday. Janet and I were still good friends but, as I expected, she had already found a new boyfriend. When she gave me a lift to the station in her car, I was now sat in the back, rather than next to her in the front seat which used to be my place.

It was difficult seeing Janet with another guy but that did not stop me visiting York again in the February holiday. I arranged to have a drink in the college bar with old friends, Peter and Jane. Their friend, Pauline, came along with them. I had seen Pauline occasionally when she been working with Jane in the library. They both studied History. That evening, I got to know her better and found we had much in common. She was even interested in football having been a City season ticket holder, albeit the wrong City. She was a Manchester City fan. Jane later remarked to Pauline that she knew that Pauline was interested in me as she laughed at my jokes! Quite appropriately, it was St Valentine's Day. The next evening, there was the weekly pub quiz at The Charles in Heslington. Peter, Jane and Pauline had been to the quiz before but had not had much success. This time, with my help, their team came first and won four pints of beer each. I would not be able to share the prize as I was due to travel home the next day. I did have my eye on a greater prize, however, and my chance came later when I offered to walk Pauline back to her lodgings. It was one of the best walks I have ever had. We spent a few hours together in her student house before agreeing to meet up the next morning. We only had a little time together before I had to go to the station and make the long journey back to Ledbury. On the way, I thought about the events of my trip to York and that I had finally found the woman who would eventually become my wife. It seems that my time with Carol (living apart for two years whilst we dated) and Janet (a Mancunian) had been preparation for my life with Pauline (a Mancunian who, as it turned out, would live a long way from me for four years).

For the rest of Pauline's final year at York, I would try to get up north as often as I could. That Summer, we spent much time together in Manchester and on a caravan holiday in Anglesey. Pauline then went to Bristol to train to be a nursery teacher. Bristol was only two train rides away from Ledbury, when the trains were running properly, so it was easier to get to see her. She was living in a bedsit and her landlady was Polly Lloyd, a presenter on BBC Radio Bristol. Pauline then got her first job in Plymouth. She was moving further away from me! It was quite a strain on our relationship at times, but I managed to get down to Plymouth quite frequently as Pauline's best friend down there, Carol, had started dating Malc, a PE teacher who worked in Birmingham. Malc was able to pick me up from Tewkesbury on a Friday after school and drive us both down to Devon. We would then return first thing on Monday morning and go straight into work. I applied, without success, for a few jobs in Devon but Devon was a popular place to teach and getting a promotion was quite hard. After a few years, Pauline and I decided that we would both try to get jobs in Bristol. Bristol had a good nursery school background and we had enjoyed our time there whilst Pauline was training. Again, I was unsuccessful in trying to get a promotion post and so decided to try to make a sideways move instead. I applied for a job at Brimsham Green School in Yate, a new town about ten miles from Bristol. I got the job, and within a few days, Pauline was also successful in getting a job at Broomhill Infant School in Bristol. It was nearly four years since we had first met and we would now, at last, be living in the same place.

We decided we would rent somewhere first and, providing we could bear living with each other, we would then buy a house. When Pauline had first lived in Bristol, we had heard an advert on commercial radio for 'Fiats in Fishponds'. The thought of some Italian cars floating around in a pond had always appealed to us, so we started our search for accommodation in Fishponds. It was in the east of the city which was more convenient for me to catch a bus to Yate for work. We found a house in Charlton Road and the letting agent was impressed that we knew Polly Lloyd from local radio. Happily, Pauline and I got on well and, nine months later, moved into what would become our lifetime home in Parnall Road.

I made a big impression at my new school in that, within three years, the rest of the mathematics department had left! Not only that, but some had decided to leave teaching altogether to become, for example, a missionary and a photographer. This meant that I was able to get my promotion after all as I then became the second-in-charge in the mathematics department. I should add that three of the staff that replaced my colleagues were still teaching at the school with me thirty years later, so, I hope, it was not because of me that the others had left! A couple of years later I also became the Examinations Officer which meant another increase in salary. Initially I was able to get a lift from a colleague, Des, to school, rather than relying on the buses every day. Des played rugby in his spare time and, at the end of the season, decided that he wanted to start cycling to work to keep fit. I decided to join him and bought myself a new bike. That was a great decision as I am sure that my nine-mile bike ride each way to work helped maintain what little sanity I had. Teaching can be very stressful, but I had usually got work out of my system by the time I had cycled home in all weathers.

Pauline and I were married in Manchester in March 1986. Simon was my best man, and I was pleased that the rest of the family successfully made the journey up north from rural Herefordshire. For Peta and her family, it was quite a journey and they arrived at the hotel late in the evening, looking a little bedraggled. The wedding was a truly memorable day of my life. A few years later, our first son, Tom, was born in 1989, followed by Michael in 1991. Most of my spare time was taken up raising the children. We went on holiday to Pembrokeshire twice each year; to the south of the county at Easter and to the north each October half-term holiday. The Pembrokeshire holidays were very special and a great way to get away from the rigours of work. Tom and Michael's first flight in an aeroplane was when we went on holiday on the Isle of Man with Pauline's parents. For both, it would be the first of many flights around the world and aeroplanes would play a large part in Michael's career.

Bob had died early in 2011. Towards the end of the year, my family was to suffer another loss when Pauline's father died. He had requested that his body be donated for medical research so there was over a year's delay before his funeral would take place. In the meantime, Pauline's mother decided that she no longer wished to live in the large family house and bought an apartment in an old people's residential block. She did not want anyone to have the hassle of sorting through all her things when it was her time to go. Moving to a smaller home would mean she had less stuff. Of course, there was the large task of sorting through all of Pauline's Dad's belongings and documents. Whilst clearing out the loft, Pauline came across a small suitcase which contained a few interesting documents. The most significant one was a sheet of paper containing the deeds to the burial plot of her Dad's brother, Frank. Frank was born before Pauline's Dad and had died when he was only four months old. The deeds told us the plot number of his grave in Manchester South Cemetery, so we made the short journey to the cemetery to search for the plot. The cemetery covers a large area, but it did not take very long to find the spot where Frank had been buried even though it was not marked by a stone. It meant that when Pauline's Dad eventually had his funeral, he could be united with the brother he never knew. A small gravestone was put in place to commemorate both the brothers. Whilst we were at the cemetery, Michael and I were interested to find the graves of a few of the famous people buried there, including Sir Matt Busby, manager of the Manchester United 'Busby Babes', and John Alcock, who, with Arthur Brown was the first to fly across the Atlantic Ocean. We came across a large, ornate memorial with a football which we thought was Busby's but turned out to be for a local gangster! Pauline's Mum told us he had been shot in a pub near her home only a year or two before. Apparently, hundreds of people turned out for the funeral procession. I suspect most of them were checking to see that he was really dead! Looking round the cemetery made me think about finding graves of some of my ancestors. My Dad did not have a grave as he was buried at sea and Mum's ashes were scattered under a tree without a marker on the tree. It would be good to connect with some of the Lovering family by visiting their final resting places. I was to later spend many hours wandering around cemeteries in both England and America.

'It's good, the internet'. I said this once and Michael often repeated it to me when I found something useful on the computer. Subscription to Ancestry UK had helped me trace my family tree and now I wanted to find some graves. The site I found most useful was Deceased Online.

I started with my grandfather, Leonard Brasier Lovering, who died in Paddington hospital just after the Second World War but there was nothing. I next tried great grandfather, George, who died in 1888. Success! Deceased Online informed that he was buried in Camberwell Old Cemetery in Southwark and, for a small fee, I could obtain a map of the location of the grave. I duly paid and was presented with a map of the cemetery, but the 'location' covered a rather large area. I travelled to London occasionally to watch York City matches. On my next trip, I caught the train to Honor Oak station and walked up to the cemetery. It was a lovely sunny day, and I was quite happy to spend an hour or so wandering around the area indicated on my map looking for my grandfather's grave. The birds were singing to brighten the day further but, no matter hard I looked, I could not find the grave. Some of the stones were quite worn, some areas were a little overgrown and, of course, there was a good possibility that George did not have a stone at all. A little disappointed, I decided to leave the cemetery but then glimpsed where the bird song I had heard was coming from. A brightly coloured parakeet flew out of a tree, and I noticed there were several of them looking down on me. I bet they knew where the grave was!

Continuing my search online, I discovered that my great-great-grandmother, Elizabeth, wife of Joseph Lovering, had died in 1831 and was buried in Mortlake Church. Mortlake meant the end of the Oxford v Cambridge boat race to me and sure enough, as I walked along the bank of the River Thames, an eight rowed passed me. The church was quite small but a beautiful gem of a building. There was something going on in the church, with tea and cakes for sale, so I was able to ask someone about Elizabeth. She directed me to another lady who knew about these things in the church. Unfortunately, that lady was not aware of anyone of that name being buried in the church. I enjoyed having a good look round the church and its grounds, so the journey was not wasted even though, once again, it ended without a successful outcome.

Next on my list of potential gravestones was William Lovering, brother of my great-great-great grandfather who had died in 1796. The grave was near Gloucester. The dates were not quite right so I suspected that this was not the person I was after, but the grave was relatively close to my home. By now, I was desperate just to see a Lovering grave of any sort. I caught the train to Gloucester, with my bike on board, and then cycled to the small village of Sandhurst, a few miles out of the city. Conveniently, there was a map by the gate indicating where various graves were. The one for William was quite a grand memorial, just outside the church door. The wording was quite worn but I was clearly able to make out the words of the deceased, William Lovering. Some sort of success, at last. I had found a Lovering grave.

Through Ancestry UK, I had linked up with other people who were interested in the Lovering family. One of those, whose username was DennisMac, was able to provide me with a map of the Spitalfields area in London which indicated various locations relating to my family in the 18th and 19th centuries. It included places where they lived and, also the location of a tailor's shop run by the son of

Joseph Lovering, my great-great-grandfather. The focus of the map, however, was Christ Church with St Mary and St Stephen, where not only was Joseph buried, but also where his son, also Joseph, was baptised and married. Several of his children were also baptised there. I had to visit Spitalfields to walk in the steps of my ancestors. Obviously, the area had changed greatly since the days of both Josephs but many of the streets still existed. The church was a rather grand building, sitting opposite Spitalfields Market. Sadly, there was very little ground surrounding the building and no sign of any graves. Also, the church was only open on Sundays, so I was unable to explore inside.

Another contributor to Ancestry UK, Gill, was, in fact, researching the Maddison-Roberts family which had a branch linking to my family through the Grindlay sisters. My grandfather, Leonard had married Catherine (Kate) Grindlay. What I had not appreciated was that his brother, Herbert, had married Kate's sister, Clara. They had three sons, Walter, Leonard and James. Sadly, Herbert and Clara died at a very young age, possibly of cholera, along with their two eldest sons. Mary Grindlay, another sister, looked after James, the youngest orphaned child, and he grew up with Maddison-Roberts family. Gill also provided me with some photos, including one of James, who bore a remarkable resemblance to the old movie star, Stan Laurel!

All this information had sparked an interest in my grandparents and great-grandparents and their siblings. I started following their branches of the family tree

forwards to look for my cousins, twice removed, or
whatever. I came across one branch of the Lovering
family which led to two children that were born in Bristol,
my home city. Could it be that I had cousins living
nearby? I did some research and discovered that Brian
Lovering lived in Over, a small village a few miles north
of Bristol. Brian's great-grandfather was, in fact, Herbert,
my grandfather's brother. Herbert's son, James, who had
been orphaned, married Daisy Drury and had two
children. The youngest, Kenneth, was Brian's father. I
managed to contact Brian and arranged to meet him at his
house the following Sunday. It was a pleasantly warm
day, and it took me about an hour to make a leisurely ride
on my bike to Over. As I approached Brian's house, I
could see it was in a quite wealthy neighbourhood
overlooking a golf course. Simon would have liked it
there! As I went to knock on the door, I was wondering
whether there would be any family likenesses. I was
warmly greeted by Brian who was keen to find out about
my side of the family. He too had been curious to look for
any family resemblances in me. We could not detect
anything obvious. Brian was semi-retired from managing
an international food company, Lovering Foods. He had
also done research on the family tree but was not really
aware of my Dad's family. This was due to the fact that
Dad was born after the census of 1911. The census, which
is taken every ten years, is a valuable source of family
information for genealogists but is only released to the
public after 100 years. Thus, the most recent one available
was the 1911 census which lists my grandfather, Leonard,
only having three children. It did not list my Dad who
would be born two years later. Brian was pleased to be

able to add more information to his tree and was particularly fascinated by the story of my Mum and Marie Cremin. Unfortunately, he was not able to shed any light on the mystery. He was, however, aware that Dad's two eldest brothers had emigrated to Canada. The second eldest son of my grandfather, Herbert, had sailed to Canada before the War. The eldest, also called Leonard, had married and had a son called Barry. He did not emigrate to Canada with his family until after the War. I had come across a few Loverings in Canada via Facebook. Was there a chance they might be related to my grandfather's children and, consequently, me? I would need to do some more research. It had been an enjoyable afternoon chatting with Brian and his wife. It was the first time I had met a Lovering relative who was not one of my siblings or one of their children.

When I got home, I re-read some of the information I had gleaned from my Ancestry UK links and, of course, from my nephew, Tim, who had provided lots of valuable stories of the Lovering past. Gill, who told me about the Grindlay sisters, also recalled a story from her own life. She wrote, 'I remember staying every Summer holiday in Ken Lovering's bungalow (James and Daisy's son) in Dymchurch. My father had been going there since he was two years old. He is now 76'. Ken was Brian's father!

From another contact, I got a little more detail about Dad's two eldest brothers. Herbert had sailed from Southampton to Halifax in 1923. Leonard was married in 1943 and son Barry born the following year in Croydon. Leonard sailed from Liverpool to Montreal in 1954 and, according to the person who sent me the information, he was married at least three times in the UK and once in Canada!

Simon and Colin both had friends on Facebook who were Loverings from all over the world. I was keen to get to know some of these Lovering families and find out if we shared any relatives. I made friend requests with several of them and then decided it would be a good idea to set up a Facebook group just for Loverings. Consequently, The Lovering Group was created to try to link members of the Lovering family from around the world. One of those members, Dale Lovering, lived in Canada and was desperate to try to extend his family tree. He had traced his ancestors to The Red Lion pub in St Columb in Cornwall but had got stuck. Unfortunately, no-one was able to help him. It crossed my mind that my branch of the family originated in Devon, over the border from Cornwall, and that, maybe, Dale was related to one of my uncles who had emigrated to Canada. My research suggested this was not the case, but I was quite excited to be in communication with another Lovering. The internet is good!

Jeff Lovering, from New York, also joined The Lovering Group. He posted a picture of the grave of George Mason Lovering (1832-1919). George was from Massachusetts and was awarded the Medal of Honour during the American Civil War. Simon bragged that he must be a descendant of George as he was a hero. Simon also suggested that he was from a different branch of the family to the rest of us, so we were not related to George.

I looked up the family tree for George Mason Lovering and was able to trace his family back to England. Amongst his ancestors were Sir Thomas Louvering who died in 1665, who, in turn, was the son of Sir Nathan Louvering. This pleased Simon even more. Using Ancestry, I had tried tracking our actual family tree further back and came across some references to Edward I, although I was unable to establish any hard facts regarding the possible link. Maybe, Simon was right after all and we were descended from landed gentry, or even royalty! From then on, Simon always referred to the Earl of Oxford as his ancestor and it became a bit of a family joke. I managed to find a photo of George Mason Lovering and was in for a bit of a surprise. George bore an uncanny likeness to brother Bob. Was he related to us, after all?

Through Ancestry UK, I was able to track my family line back to the 15th century, on my father's side. On my mother's side, I could not even trace it back to my mum! Despite my efforts, we were no nearer solving the mystery of her identity.

2012 was quite a momentous year for me. My beloved football team, York City, played at Wembley twice within eight days and won both the F.A. Trophy and a place back in the Football League. The other big occasion was when Pauline and I went to Cambridge to see Tom's Graduation ceremony. He had achieved a First in Mathematics and had gained a place at Harvard in the U.S. to study for his PhD. It was an emotional day when we saw Tom fly from Heathrow Airport to his new life across the Atlantic

Ocean. The following Easter, it was our turn to go to Heathrow Airport to catch a flight for our first ever visit to the United States. It was a place that we had not had any great desire to visit before but, once we got there, we fell in love with Boston. It was a city not unlike Bristol, not too big and full of history. We had heard of the Boston Tea Party but there was so much more to find out about the American War of Independence. We caught the commuter train out to Concord to visit the site of one of the earliest engagements of the Revolution. We followed the Freedom Trail from Bunker Hill to Boston Common. I was able to 'say hello to Paul Revere' – a line from my favourite song about Boston; *'Back to Boston'* by Jesse Hanson. Paul Revere was buried in the Old Granary Burial Ground in the heart of Boston, where, incidentally, Esther Lovering was also buried. A Lovering grave! The information board stated that 'Esther (c 1772-1798) had married Joseph Lovering Jr, from Roxbury, a tallow chandler and died at the age of 26'. We also learned that there had been a Professor Lovering at Harvard College and that one of the buildings on the campus was named after him. In fact, it appeared that there had been many Loverings in Massachusetts which I guess was not too surprising given the Pilgrim Fathers sailed from Plymouth. Devon, along with parts of South Wales seemed to be the main areas of Lovering concentration in the UK.

Seeing Esther's grave in the Old Granary Burial Ground had made me want to find more Lovering graves. I remembered the photo of American Civil War hero George Mason Lovering's grave and looked up where it was located. To my delight, I found it was a short train ride out of Boston to the Randolph/Holbrook suburb. I travelled alone on a rather dull, cloudy day and walked about a mile from the station to the Union Cemetery. It was quite a large cemetery, but I recalled that George's grave was flanked by two stars and stripes flags and that there were trees in the background. I headed for the edge of the cemetery where there were some trees and, after a little searching, found some Lovering graves, including a Mason Lovering, but not George's. I took some photos of these graves. I wandered round more of the cemetery, looking at the inscriptions carefully, and also looking for signs of two American flags. Still no luck but, at least, the weather was improving; indeed, the sun came out. I decided that I would return to the Lovering graves and take the photos again. Now the sun was shining, it would be easier to read the inscriptions. As I approached the graves, I suddenly noticed George Mason's grave in the row behind them. How did I miss it? I was delighted to have found it and took more photos. When I got back to our apartment, I showed Pauline the pictures. I noticed that in the first set I took, you can see George Mason's grave in the background. I would have been very annoyed if I had missed it and not found it when I returned in the sunshine.

The following year, we stayed in an apartment next to the Massachusetts State House. The apartment block used to be a hotel and John F. Kennedy often stayed there. Did he stay in our apartment, I wondered? Although it was quite chilly, we enjoyed sitting on the rooftop terrace, overlooking the State House and Boston Common,

drinking tea. I was using the internet on my iPad to
research more about Lovering people from Boston. It
turned out that a Joseph Lovering had taken part in the
Boston Tea Party. He was only fourteen years old at the
time and had spotted that something seemed to be going
on and tagged along. Although he may not have played a
major part in the protest, a Lovering was involved in the
incident that led to Britain losing the United States. I also
found out that Joseph was buried in Forest Hills
Cemetery, a ride on the 'T' train to the end of the Orange
Line. As I was about to tell Pauline this discovery, a
peregrine falcon landed on the rooftop terrace, about three
metres behind her. Before I had a chance to take a picture
of it, it had flown away. Pauline caught a glimpse of it,
having initially thought that it was a gull! After that
exciting incident, I headed to the nearest 'T' station and
got the train to Forest Hills. The cemetery was set in
woodland and looked even more stunning as there was
still a few inches on snow on the ground. It was another
huge cemetery. Luckily, I spotted that the site office near
the entrance was open. I explained to the people in the
office that I was looking for the grave of Joseph Lovering,
who had witnessed the events in Boston Harbour in 1773.
They were quite surprised as they had not realised that
they had someone involved in the Boston Tea Party in
their cemetery! They checked their records and found
Joseph's grave. There were, in fact, several Lovering
graves along with graves of the Gay family. They kindly
marked the location of the graves on a map, so I was
quickly able to find them. It was not too far from the
entrance to the cemetery. I was getting used to seeing the
Lovering name on a grave and this one had some

historical importance.

Later that week, Pauline and I caught the bus from Boston for the long drive to Provincetown on Cape Cod. After checking into our bed and breakfast accommodation, we went to explore the town. As it was early April, the resort was very quiet. In the summer, it is the gay capital of Massachusetts. There is also a site nearby where the first settlers to the United States landed on the continent. The town is dominated by a large tower, the Pilgrim Memorial Monument, which was built to commemorate the landing of the settlers. We headed to the tower first and made the ascent to the top for the glorious views. We then visited the small museum at the base of the tower. As we looked at the exhibits, many about the whaling industry, I got quite excited and called Pauline over. There was a stars and stripes flag and the inscription that had been used to drape the podium during the Laying of the Cornerstone ceremony in 1907. President Theodore Roosevelt had led the ceremony but, amongst the guests, was Congressman Lovering! I was finding Loverings everywhere.

2016 was my 'annus horribilis' and not only because my football team, York City, were relegated from the Football League again. A week or so after City's demise, it was my turn to fall from grace as I was hit by a car on my way to work. I had now been working at Brimsham Green School for over thirty years and for nearly all that time, I cycled the nine miles to work every day. Most of my route was now on traffic-free cycle paths so it was usually a very pleasant journey to and from work. Indeed, the bike rides at the end of the day were a great way of releasing any tension that may have built up after a tough day trying to make youngsters enjoy mathematics. By the time I got home, I would be very relaxed once again, with school out of my system. On several days each week, a colleague, Bob Chapman, cycled home with me and we were able to have a good moan about how bad our day had been, it was very therapeutic. Cycling to work also helped maintain my health and I had only had about six days off work for illness in the previous twenty-five years. I had, however, been forced off work due to injury, rather than poor health. The first time was when I got knocked off my bike by a pedestrian who stepped out into the road in front of me. It was a Saturday evening, six years previously in 2010, and I was riding home from the station after witnessing yet another York City defeat. I managed to walk home but my chest was very sore. Pauline was away for the weekend, so I got a taxi to Frenchay Hospital to have it checked. I was told that I had probably cracked or bruised a rib. There was no point in taking an x-ray as they would not be able to do anything. The cure is just to let it heal itself. They made sure that there was no damage to my lungs, which can sometimes be pierced by a broken rib, and I was on my way home, still in much discomfort. I had to take a week off school before I was fit enough to return though it took several weeks before I was able to sleep comfortably.

This time, it was a lovely Spring morning when I had my accident. The sun was just rising and was low in the sky. I reached the end of the cycle path and joined the road that passes through the small village of Westerleigh, on my journey to work. As I reached the top of the hill and went around a corner, I was aware of a vehicle very close to me. The next moment, I felt a thud on my right as I was hit by something and began to fall to the ground. It all seemed to happen in slow motion as I prepared to break my fall with my hands which hit the tarmac very forcefully. I was very shaken and winded as I managed to get up and sit on the kerb. The driver of the car that had hit me had stopped and he came to see how I was. I gestured that I was trying to get my breath and could not speak for a moment. As I tried to recover, I looked at my bike laying in the middle of the road and tried to see if there was much damage. I think I was more worried about the bike than about myself. I noticed something near the bike and could not figure out what it was. The driver then pointed to it and said that it was his wing mirror. I guessed it was that wing mirror that had hit me. I felt a little satisfaction, despite my agony, that at least the car had suffered too. The driver explained that he was blinded by the sun and asked if he should call an ambulance. I declined the offer. As usual, I did not want a fuss. I took his details and told him I would be all right. I phoned Pauline to tell her what had happened, and she said she would come and collect me. I struggled to pick up the bike and inspect the damage. The bike was not too bad, just a slightly buckled wheel and a bent pedal. Certainly, better than me. My hands were badly bruised and my legs were bleeding. I was also very sore where the car had hit me. I knew Bob would be along soon on his bike and I was able to move to a place where Pauline would be able park the car. By now the adrenalin rush was fading and I was beginning to feel very weak. It was a relief when I saw

Bob approaching. I could tell by his shocked expression that I must have looked a mess. I described to him what had happened and asked him for a piece of paper. 'What for?', he enquired. 'So, I can write down the cover work for my lessons today!'. I was, as ever, the true professional and wanted to ensure my students did not suffer through my absence! Pauline arrived, and Bob helped me and my bike into the car.

When I got home, Pauline sat me on a chair, so she could clean my wounds. She told me not to sit on the sofa as it was too low, and I wouldn't be able to get up again. She was right. After a few minutes, I felt quite woozy and said I had to lie down. I lay on the sofa, still in extreme discomfort. I talked to a doctor over the telephone and he prescribed some painkillers. After about two hours on the sofa, I needed to go to the toilet. I could not get up. Pauline tried to help but I was still unable to move. Because my hands were bruised, I could not grip anything, and I was in extreme pain when I moved anyway. I did eventually fight the pain and made it to the bathroom. The painkillers did their job initially but, unfortunately, I threw them up again soon afterwards. I was not used to taking medicine. I spent over a week sleeping upright on cushions on the sofa as it was too painful to lie down. It gave me time to think about my future and consider the possibility of retiring earlier than planned. I was put off the thought a little by the passing of the day, sat on the sofa. In the morning, I would watch the children pass the window on their way to school. Seven hours later, they would pass the other way on their way home. Is this what it is like to retire? I also thought a great deal about the family. I had time to think through all the mysteries surrounding Mum and Dad, wondering whether we would ever solve the mystery. Bob had died a few years earlier and it could easily have been me being killed this time. I thought a lot about mortality. I was keen to get back to work and probably returned too soon, but I could not face many more days alone at home. I think my students were pleased to see me again although there was a comment from one of them. 'Sir, you know that work you set us when you had your accident? Well, it didn't really make sense'.

I was not the only one in the family that was having issues with my health. Simon had been diagnosed with diabetes a few years earlier and he had lost a lot of weight in that time. As always, he diverted attention from himself and would comment on how I had seemed to put on weight. More recently, however, he had been having other problems, including difficulties with his breathing. Simon had smoked all his adult life, so he feared that he may even have cancer. Pauline and I went to Worcester to visit Simon and Karen and stay overnight with them. When we arrived, we found Simon was in a relaxed mood. He was relieved to have heard that he did not have cancer after all, although the doctors were still not sure what was wrong with him. He would have to take more tests. You could tell that this was a huge weight off his shoulders although he was not out of the woods yet. Simon did not want to focus too much on his health as he did not want people fussing over him. He had other issues on his mind that were upsetting him. He could not believe that the recent Referendum for membership of the European Union had resulted in a vote for the UK to leave. He complained about the Little Englanders who were yearning for a Britain of the past. Simon was also very saddened that our nephew, Matt, had left his wife, Claire, just a few months after the birth of their son, Fred. On a happier note, Simon told us of his trip to Wembley to watch Hereford play in the FA Vase Final. It was the club's first trip to Wembley but, unfortunately, they lost 1-4 to Morpeth. It was a remarkable achievement to even reach Wembley, given it was the first season back as a brand new 'phoenix' team. The original Hereford United had encountered financial problems and was dissolved. The new Hereford team, whose motto is 'Forever United', was able to remain at the old Hereford United ground at Edgar Street. The new club started life several tiers below where the previous club played in non-league football and then gained promotion in the first season. Apart from the football chat, we also had our regular conversation about the Lovering mystery and came up with new possibilities for the identity of Mum. Perhaps she was a relative of the Earl of Oxford! It was all speculation, of course, and we were basically reaching the conclusion that the Lovering mystery would remain just that. A mystery. Simon discussed his future and that he might have to give up his work if his health did not improve. He had already decided to play less golf as I think he wanted no-one to know that he was not well. Both Simon and Karen had each notched over a hundred countries visited on their travels around the world. They had decided that they would make just one more long-haul journey abroad. Karen had loved Bali when they visited it previously, so they were going to return there in a couple of months, at the end of October. It might also give Simon an opportunity to see the Komodo Dragon. As children, we had been fascinated by a David Attenborough documentary on television, in black and white, of course, about the giant lizard. It had made a big impression on us. I was now fully recovered from my bike accident, but Simon impressed on me to ensure that I had regular medical check-ups. I was enjoying my cup of tea when, suddenly, Simon grabbed my arm and attached an arm band. He started pumping the arm band. He was checking my blood pressure! He announced that my blood pressure was fine, but he now needed to check my blood sugar levels. This involved him pricking my finger to obtain a sample of my blood. He tested it and stated that my blood sugar levels were also all right. I was pleased to be declared fit and healthy despite being physically assaulted by Doctor Simon. The four of us enjoyed a delicious Indian meal that evening. It had been delightful to enjoy some quality time with both Simon and Karen.

Simon had not really celebrated his 60th birthday but Karen decided to put that right for his 61st birthday coming up in October. She invited Colin and me to meet up in London and go out for a meal. We had hoped to go to the theatre as well, but that was not possible due to work. Karen had, however, booked tickets for herself and Simon to see 'Les Miserables', Simon's favourite show. Pauline and I booked train tickets and a hotel close to the Olympic Stadium in Stratford, east London, near to where Simon and Karen were staying. A week later, we received a phone call from Karen to say that, following early tests, it appeared that Simon may have motor neurone disease.

More tests needed to be done to confirm it. I was devastated to hear the news. I did not know much about the illness but immediately thought of Stephen Hawking, the only other person I knew that had it. Would Simon end up like him; in a wheelchair and having to rely on an artificial voice to communicate with us? I looked up more information on the internet. It appeared that it was a very unpredictable ailment which could debilitate the body within weeks or take several years. The site included a useful video by someone who had it, entitled '*Coping with Motor Neurone Disease*'. It offered a more optimistic quality of life with the disease, that is, until I reached the end. It informed the viewer that the person had subsequently died since making the video. It was too hard to contemplate what life was like for Simon. Karen told us that he did not want other people to know of his condition, including the rest of the family, apart from Colin.

Pauline and I travelled down to London on the train and agreed to meet up with Colin in Foyles bookshop on Charing Cross Road. Colin had flown over from Romania and was full of cold. We then went to the Cambridge pub where we had agreed to meet Karen. She had left Simon in a coffee shop whilst she told us her plans. Simon was completely unaware that his brothers were going to share the weekend with him. We sat at a table in the corner of the pub which was, by now, quite busy. Karen went to collect Simon, who, when they arrived at the pub, was a little dismayed to see how busy it was. Karen spotted some seats and suggested that they sit at that table. "I don't really want to share a table with other people", was

Simon's response, not knowing that it was his brothers that were sitting at the table. We were pretending to look at the pictures on the wall and then turned around to greet Simon. It was a very emotional moment for all of us, but particularly Simon, who was moved to tears. It was the first time we had seen Simon since his provisional diagnosis of motor neurone disease, and he looked noticeably weaker. After chatting and drinking for an hour, we headed for our hotels and agreed to meet in Stratford for the evening meal. Colin was not too happy as he had booked into a hotel in Acton in west London – the other side of the city to Stratford.

Michael had been staying in Watford and decided he would join us for our meal in Stratford. We met Karen and Simon and waited at the station for Michael to arrive. After a few minutes, we noticed that Simon had sat on a wall and was talking to an old man. The man turned out to be a West Ham United fan and they were reminiscing about the Hereford United glory days of the seventies when Hereford met West Ham in the FA Cup. It was typical of Simon that he could strike up a rapport with a total stranger and become friends within a few minutes. We greeted Michael and headed to the shopping centre to look for a restaurant. There was a lift to the shopping centre. Unfortunately, the lift was out of order. You could see Simon's spirits visibly drop. He would have to use the stairs instead and it was then we realised just how weak Simon was. He needed plenty of help from us to make it to the top. We found a nice Italian restaurant and were joined, eventually, by Colin who had travelled across the city and was a little weary due to his travels and his cold.

Despite his earlier struggle to get to the restaurant, Simon was in top form during the meal. He joked with the waiters, was full of great stories and you would not know that he had found it difficult to get about all day. Surprisingly, Simon also stated that he had not enjoyed the performance of 'Les Miserables' as much as he had previously. Even Colin was cheered by the jollity of the evening. The following morning, Pauline and I checked out of our hotel and walked the half mile or so to Simon and Karen's hotel. It was now Simon's birthday, so it was great to be able to share it with him over a cup of tea. It was also quite amusing to watch him trying to manoeuvre his large car out of the hotel car park. We waved them off and then went for a stroll round the Olympic Park before heading home ourselves.

I had planned to visit Simon and Karen after they got back from their trip to the Far East. The Saturday that I was free was approaching but I was full of cold so not feeling great. I checked the train times to Worcester and found that, due to engineering works, there was a rail replacement bus service running instead. I didn't fancy a long bus ride so opted to visit them on a later date. The following Monday evening, I received a text from Colin saying that he could not get hold of either Simon or Karen and was concerned. I tried phoning them but there was no reply. It did seem rather strange. Since I left for work before six o'clock in the morning, I decided I would try again after work. After I got home, I was just changing out of my cycling clothes, when the phone rang. It was Peta.

"Have you heard about Simon?", she said. My immediate thought was that she had found out about him possibly having motor neurone disease. She was sure to discover that eventually.

"No, what?", I responded.

"He's dead!"

Now my brain was in a complete mess. I knew that there might be something up after Colin's message, but I was not expecting this.

"What! What happened?"

"He collapsed last night and was taken to hospital. He died a little later.", Peta said, in a broken voice, and went on to say that she didn't know any more.

I was numb with shock. I just could not believe that this had happened. It was a blow when Mum and Bob died, but Simon was the brother I was probably closest to, along with Colin. Simon was only two years older than me. Just sixty-one years old, the same age that Bob died. I rang Colin and spoke to him briefly. I could tell that he was devastated by the news and, like me, could not really accept that Simon was no longer with us. Colin and Simon had become particularly close in recent years through their travels together and with Simon offering brotherly support when Colin was having personal crises. I spent the rest of the evening, indeed the next few weeks, just thinking about Simon. I could hear his voice, expressing his thoughts on the news, family, travelling and so on. I also looked up old photos of him and posted one a day on

Facebook. I guess it was my way of coming to terms with the fact we had lost him. The family tree had not only lost another leaf. It was more like it had lost a branch. I then thought of the adventurous Simon climbing the tree in our garden in Eastnor, fifty years before. I had warned him about stepping on to that branch. Now that branch, not of the tree, but of the family, had snapped and fallen.

A few days later, Pauline and I visited Karen in Worcester to offer our support for her and to find out more of the circumstances of his death. It was very tough for Karen to relive that night, but I think it helped her in some way. Simon had been finding it difficult to breathe and had made his way downstairs to the living room. Karen had called an ambulance and was trying to comfort Simon whilst they waited for it to arrive. She could tell there was something seriously wrong with him and suspected that he did too. At one point, he asked what Yogi was doing behind Karen. Yogi, their dog, had died a few years earlier and was buried in the back garden. Was that a sign that Yogi had come to collect Simon, so they could be together again? When they got Simon to the hospital, it was clear that he was unable to breathe on his own and, eventually, the decision was made to turn off the life support. Ironically, the report came through that same day to confirm that Simon did, indeed, have motor neurone disease. The doctor described it as 'a car crash waiting to happen'. For Simon, the crash came sooner rather than later. That was probably a blessing as I know that Simon would not wanted to have been disabled and having to rely on others. A date had not yet been set for the funeral. Karen wanted to give Simon the best send-off and wanted to have the wake at the golf club. She was waiting to find out when it was available. Given that Simon was Captain of the golf club at one time, we hoped they would do all they could to fulfil Karen's wishes. Karen also told us about their final holiday in Bali. Simon had been too weak to enjoy it fully. They had spent a lot of time talking and crying together. Sadly, Simon was not able to visit and see the Komodo dragon.

The rest of the week at work was a real struggle. My mind was not on work. On Saturday, I had already booked train tickets to go to watch York City play in Bromley in Kent. When I arrived at the ground, I posted a message on Facebook saying, 'I feel like I should be at a Hereford football match today, really'. Back came replies from the family saying, 'Let's go to a Hereford game in memory of Simon'. That seemed like a great idea. I looked at the Hereford fixture list for the next home game and was pleasantly surprised to see it was against Yate Town. I had worked in Yate over thirty years and cycled past the Yate Town ground every day! Colin contacted Hereford explaining that we were coming to celebrate Simon's life as a Hereford fan. They kindly offered us tickets at a reduced price, and they said they would put something about him in the matchday programme. I duly sent them some information about Simon and included a photo of him celebrating a Hereford goal, scored against my York City!

The date for the funeral was finally sorted and it was to be the day before the Hereford game. Simon had read the eulogies at both Mum and Bob's funeral. I had not had much input into those services. This time, I had to step up to the mark. Karen asked that both Colin and I do the duty of delivering the eulogy. I suggested to Colin that I covered Simon's early life and then he could pick up from me and describe his later adventures. I intended that my speech should not be too stilted and morbid, so I would not write it out as such, but just note key points and try to speak more naturally. Karen, however, wanted to vet the speech first so I ended up typing up my contribution. It did give the opportunity for me to see what Colin intended to say. It looked like a very fitting memory of Simon and his life.

Karen asked us to perform another duty on the day. She asked that Colin and I, along with two other people, carry Simon's coffin into the church. This caused me to worry as it was obviously something I had never done before, and things could go wrong. For reassurance, I looked up information on the internet. The internet is good. On there, someone had asked a question which voiced my concern. 'Will the coffin be heavy?'. The response was that it would depend on the materials of the coffin and the weight of the person. It went on to say that there was no need to worry as there would be six of you sharing the weight. That did not help my confidence. There would only be four of us carrying Simon. Just below that item, there was a video showing what could happen. One of the pallbearers stumbled and the coffin fell to the ground. What was worse, the lid came off and the body inside is revealed! The internet was not alleviating my concerns though I supposed these worries might help ease my emotions about losing Simon, on the day of the funeral.

Those of us involved with duties met at Simon and Karen's house on the morning of the funeral. I was relieved to find out that Stef, one of Simon's best friends from the golf club, would be one of the other pall bearers. Stef had regularly worked for an undertaker and had performed the job many times before. He was able to tell us what to expect. We then travelled to the church which was near the centre of Worcester. It was set at the end of a short cul-de-sac and looked beautiful in the winter sunshine. Emotions ran high when the coffin arrived. I was still worried about making sure we got it into the church with the lid still intact. I took the weight of the back of the coffin, alongside Colin, and we carried it into the church. Apart from a nervous zig-zag motion through two doors at the entrance, we successfully placed the coffin in the centre of the aisle. The sun was shining through the windows and the pews in the church had been arranged so that everyone was facing towards the coffin. It was a wonderful service although it was very hard not to think of Simon in the coffin in front of us. Even though he had died a few weeks previously, it still had not sunk in that he had gone. I think my part of the eulogy went well and then Colin stepped up to do his bit. I noticed that he had added more to his speech- always after a little more attention! Towards the end, his voice began to falter. I stepped up next to him to offer support. He managed to get through the speech though I know it was particularly hard for him. He later told me that he thought that I was going to take over from him when I stepped up! I was quite pleased to see the undertakers lift the coffin and take it to the hearse. I thought that we had to do that, as well. We followed the hearse to the nearby cemetery. My nephews, Dan and Matt, had the onerous task of lowering the coffin into the ground. It made me realise that my job of carrying the coffin was nothing. The look on Dan's face as he lowered the coffin made everyone feel a little amused. Secretly, some of us were hoping he would fall into the grave after the coffin! Burials are grim affairs but the atmosphere was lifted by the sound of children playing loudly in a primary school, adjacent to the cemetery.

The wake was held at Gaudet Luce Golf Club as Karen had wanted and it was a wonderful celebration of Simon's life. There was a display of photos which made me appreciate all the people and friends he had met over the years. I was especially pleased to see that many of his friends from his Hereford days had been able to attend. They had many great stories to tell of the mischief that Simon occasionally got up to in his youth. Derek Redmond, the Olympic athlete that Simon and Karen had first met on their cruise across the Atlantic from New York, was also there. Tom missed the funeral service but managed to get to the cemetery and to the golf club after flying in from Boston, thanks to Michael driving him from Heathrow. Even Claire, who had only recently had the traumatic split from her husband Matt soon after the birth of their first child, was there. It must have been hard for her to be there, but she, like everyone present, held Simon in such high regard, that she just had to attend. Colin was complaining that his shoulder was sore from bearing the weight of the coffin. I commented that mine was fine. In fact, I had thought that the coffin was much lighter than I had expected. We mentioned this this to Stef, who pointed out that this often happens if one person is slightly taller than the other. We compared our shoulder heights: Colin was, indeed, a little taller than me and so had taken more than his fair share of the load.

The next day, several members of the family met in a pub in Hereford. We made our way to the football ground at Edgar Street. I bought a matchday programme and was impressed with the article that the club had included about Simon. In addition, several announcements were made over the public address regarding Simon and the fact that some of his family were present. And if that was not enough, the scoreboard regularly flashed up a message about Simon too. Hereford Football Club did a great job in honouring the memory of Simon. It did us the power of good to enjoy the football after the difficulty of burying Simon the previous day. Amongst the family attending was young Fred, Matt's son, who had been born earlier that year. I thought it was great that Hereford may have lost one fan, but here was the next generation, and Fred would become a big follower of Hereford. Unfortunately, it was not to be, and he fell asleep, despite Hereford winning the game 4-1. His mother, Claire would be happy, as she wanted him to be a rugby fan.

There was another family gathering in Hereford the following September. As Bob and Simon were keen golfers and we often played on the putting green near Hereford Cathedral, I inaugurated The Lovering Trophy. Each player did one round of the course and the lowest score won. Colin was the first winner of the small trophy I bought, with Michael and Dan in the runners-up places. Peta provided the rather exotic fruit cake which the cause of much conversation. Colin had flown in from Romania, so we took the opportunity to visit Simon's grave together. Although there was no headstone yet, Karen had erected a small plaque to mark the grave. She had also decided that, since Simon could no longer travel the world, the world would have to come to him. If any of the family travelled abroad, they were to bring a flag of that country back to place on the grave. As I stood by Simon's grave, two thoughts passed through my mind. First, I half expected to look up and see Mum, Bob and Simon in the distance watching us, as in the scene at the end of the Star Wars film when Darth Vader, Obi-Wan and Yoda watch over the burning pyre. I looked up but they weren't there. Disappointing. The other thing that occurred to me was that I had travelled over the country looking for a grave of a Lovering that was a relative of mine. I had finally found a grave, but it was not one I ever wanted to visit. I had lost another brother and was still no nearer to finding out who Mum was or what happened to Marie Cremin.

8 COLIN

Colin was born on 2nd December,1959 on, like Simon, the British Army base in Rheindahlen, West Germany. He was the youngest of the children and was always referred to as 'the baby of the family'. His stature lived up to the title as, until he was about fifteen, he was always much shorter than both Simon and me. He then had a growth spurt and caught up with us! As mentioned before, there was also the joke in the family that he was not really a Lovering. The story went that the wrong baby was brought home from the hospital when he was born. As kids, Simon and I would often refer to this whenever he was annoying us. We would say, 'You're not really a Lovering. We wish Mum and Dad had brought the right baby back instead of you!'. It was very cruel but, there were some noticeable differences between us and him. Apart from his height, he had a much fairer complexion than us and there was a hint of ginger colour in his hair. Throughout his life, Simon would often refer to Colin's 'ginger hair', just to wind him up.

Of all the children, Colin was the one who led the most

nomadic life. Even in his early days, he was moved from school to school- a contrast to my experience. When we moved from Eastnor to Ledbury, Colin changed primary schools, whilst I was allowed to remain at Eastnor. Admittedly, I only had a month or two left there so there was little point in moving to a new school for such a short time. Colin was certainly able enough to pass his 11-Plus exam but circumstances, once again, had an influence on his destiny. In those days, you had to pass the 11-Plus exam to go to the Grammar School. He passed the preliminary test and went to Ledbury Grammar School, where I was now attending, to sit the final 11-Plus exam. When he got home, we asked him how it went. He complained that one of the teachers there had been wearing strong perfume which was a little distracting for him. He failed the exam and was offered a place at Ledbury Secondary Modern School, rather than at the Grammar School. I often wonder how his life path would have changed if that French teacher had not been in the exam room that afternoon. Maybe it was meant to be that Colin did not follow the academic route and that his destiny was in the big wide world instead. We always used to say that 'every path leads somewhere'.

After a couple of years at Ledbury, Mike, Mum's new husband, got the job in Abberley and Colin was on the move again. Once again, I was allowed to continue my education at the Grammar School, but Colin had to adjust to another new school, The Chantry School, Martley, near Worcester. Colin said that he really enjoyed his time there, but his education was to be disrupted again. After Mike had set fire to the school where he worked, the family were homeless again. Colin moved into the caravan at Bromsberrow and returned to Ledbury Secondary School. He felt like an outsider on his return and did not enjoy the experience. It was hardly surprising that he was not particularly successful in his exams, but he did secure a place at Hereford Art College. Unfortunately, just like his older brother Bob who was also a gifted artist, things did not go well for Colin. His hopes of becoming a Graphic Designer were fading. He left college and got a job with a local firm called Almont Plastics. Plastic and plastic packaging was to be a major part of his life for the next twenty or thirty years.

Colin was now living with Mum in the council flat in Lawnside Road in Ledbury but, that too, was not to last long. He had met Debra Smith and they were to be married and live in their own home. The wedding took place at the main church in Ledbury and was followed by a reception at The Royal Oak pub. The reception was to be followed by a disco in the evening. Colin and Debra had chosen to get married on the day that Sebastian Coe was racing against his arch-rival, and fellow Briton, Steve Ovett, in the Moscow Olympics. It was a long-anticipated meeting of the two middle distance giants of athletics. The Lovering family was sport mad and did not want to miss the race, even though it was Colin's big day. We apologised to him and said we would nip home to watch it on television and then return to his celebrations afterwards as soon as possible. We were all feeling a little guilty about deserting the baby of the family on his wedding day. That was until Colin also decided he wanted to watch the race too and joined us!

In the next two years, Colin became father to two boys, Daniel and Matthew, whom he adored. His work was taking him away from home a lot and, over the years, he and Debra drifted apart, and relations became strained. Eventually they decided, very amicably, that it would be best if they separated. Living in a small town like Ledbury, there was inevitably some malicious talk about Colin and Debra, but they both managed the split well. Daniel and Matthew saw a great deal of their father still, despite their parents' eventual divorce. For some time, Colin was living in Bristol and the boys would often visit him. He was living next door to Billy Clark, a player of one of the local Football League teams, Bristol Rovers, so Colin would take them to watch The Gas play. 'The Gas' is a nickname for Bristol Rovers, whose old ground in Eastville was next to some gasometers. Dan's early encounter with Bristol Rovers led him to becoming a big fan, a Gashead, much to his regret! Matt did not succumb to The Gas, and later became a regular visitor to Aston Villa games. Despite always being on Bob's Ipswich team when we used to play football in the field by our house in Eastnor, Colin developed into a supporter of the opposition of those games. Like our Dad, he became a Tottenham Hotspur fan.

Colin's job eventually found him living in Burton Latimer in Northamptonshire. He got to know his next-door neighbour rather well. So well, in fact, that he married her! Colin's wedding to Sami was on Mum's birthday, nearly twenty years after his first marriage. The wedding reception was held at the local cricket club and most of the family made the journey to Northamptonshire.

Unfortunately, Mum was not able to be there, but she heard some of the speeches via the phone. There were, in fact, quite a few speeches as many of Sami's family wanted to say something. It was obvious that her family were highly regarded in the local community and that they were a close-knit group.

Life did not stand still for Colin and his performance and success for his company led to him becoming the manager of sales over a large area. His operations moved to Europe, so it was natural that he and Sami would eventually move to the continent. They found themselves living in a lovely house in the rather remote countryside of Northern France. They got on well with the locals in the nearby village and it appeared to be an idyllic place to live. It was quite an adventure when Pauline and I visited them with Tom and Michael. We caught the overnight ferry from Portsmouth to Le Havre, having travelled by train from Bristol. It was quite strange being on the dockside at Le Havre at the crack of dawn and making our way to the railway station. We got a train to Rouen, although the ticket inspector seemed to suggest that we had the wrong ticket. He let us travel anyway. Colin met us in Rouen and drove us to the house where we were greeted by Simon and Karen, who were also staying for the weekend. It was a very special time there, partly because it was rare for the three youngest brothers to spend time away together.

Residing in France was quite short-lived as Colin's career continued to dominate his life and he was offered a global training position in the USA. This was another part of his adventure but also the start of the end of his marriage. It was a long way from Northamptonshire and relations between Colin and Sami became difficult. Things came to a head when some large debts were run up on credit cards and the financial position became quite grim as did the relationship.

After a couple of years, Colin received another offer within the company he worked for and returned to the UK, in Bradford, to manage a new acquisition. Colin and Sami eventually got divorced and Colin was officially on his own again. After three more years, he felt ready to make a fresh start and take up a new challenge as an independent business performance consultant to make use of the business skills and knowledge that he had gained over many years. He decided that he would move away from the UK. There were some options in the USA and elsewhere, but he ended up working as an associate consultant with a company in Bucharest, Romania. Romania was recovering from the trauma of the 1989 Revolution and the fall of Ceaucescu and communism. Membership of the European Community would offer many opportunities for developing businesses in the country and Colin would be there to offer advice and training. Colin moved to Romania around the time that Mum died and it would be many years before I visited him in Bucharest. Simon once suggested that he and I should visit Colin out there so the three brothers could be together again. It never happened and it is something that I regret.

The death of Simon had a big effect on both Colin and

me. We made more of an effort to keep in touch with each other. I was approaching my sixtieth birthday, so thoughts of retirement were entering my head. I had, at one time, expected to carry on teaching well beyond sixty, but my bike accident and Simon dying made me re-assess my position.

For Colin it was a mixed bag of emotion as Simon's passing coincided with him meeting Corina. Colin always felt that Simon's influence played a part in this since he was always nagging him to "find yourself a decent woman for God's sake!". Corina turned out to be the transformation and settling down of Colin's turbulent, ever-changing life that he needed.

Colin and Corina married in May 2019. It was a special and somewhat poignant moment in his life as Dan and Matthew recalled, in their best men speech, the influence that Simon had on them and their father. I'm sure that Corina took up the coaching role gap left by Simon's passing and we were all delighted to see Colin so settled and happy!

With Corina's great support, he built a successful consulting business along with writing a book about his life in sales entitled "The Day in the Life of Exceptional sales Professionals" selling over 5,000 copies worldwide.

I had decided that I would retire at Christmas, just after reaching retirement age, so I could enjoy a life away from work – something that neither Bob nor Simon were able to do. Circumstances changed, however. Due to the government's austerity measures, budgets in schools were being cut to the bone. My school was no exception and redundancies would be required within my department. I applied for voluntary redundancy, but I was unsuccessful. As I had worked there for nearly a third of a century, it would have been far too expensive to make me redundant. I felt that it was time to go so I decided I would finish in the Summer, instead of waiting until Christmas. It would mean that I had no income until I reached my pension age in November. In the end, I carried on teaching one day each week part-time so I could complete teaching the A level Further Maths course, which was finishing the following Summer. It was a wise decision as it would mean I would not suddenly stop working. I would still have contact with my old colleagues, have a little income and I would also have more time to do things I wanted to do. I had started teaching myself how to play the piano and I renewed my subscription to Ancestry UK. I was determined to try and get to the bottom of the mystery of the family somehow. The only problem was that it was now 35 years since I started on this journey to find out the truth about Mum. By then, the people who might know who Mum was were probably no longer with us. In all honesty, we had made very little progress in all that time despite finding out things about other members of the family and other Loverings.

When I had a spare moment sat at the computer, I would use Ancestry UK to do random searches for people called Helen, born in London in the 1920s. There would be lots of results and I would study the list of Cambridge rugby blues to see if any names matched. Of course, there was a very good chance that Mum was not even born in London.

Given her stories of travel around the world, she may well have been born somewhere overseas and those would not appear in my searches. Maybe, I would have to fork out more money to get the worldwide subscription. Given that there were not many people still alive that might solve the mystery, I felt the internet was the only likely solution to getting to the answer. My nephew, Tim, had done much research into the Lovering family tree and it was him that had got me into Ancestry in the first place. He had produced a quite detailed family tree for the Lovering side of the family and I knew that he was as keen as me to solve the mystery of Mum's origins. Tim was now working in the Middle East and I only heard from him occasionally, with updates on his family and the odd story about a Lovering ancestor. My searches on Ancestry were not very productive and I was beginning to lose hope when I received this message from Tim:

'I thought I'd drop you a line because I recently got Jan to do an Ancestry.com DNA test and got some amazing results back in terms of proving previously tenuous relationships. More interestingly I was able to identify some pretty close relatives with no paper evidence trail at all. I was wondering if you had done or considered doing this? I was sceptical before, but having seen what it can do I think there is a fair chance it could shed some light on our big gap'

I had seen adverts for Ancestry DNA but not really thought anymore about it. It seemed that Tim was also doubtful about it but the results he got for Jan, his mother, changed his mind. At last, this seemed like a great way to find some links to Mum's family and, maybe, pin down who she really was. I went to the website to get more information. Basically, they collected samples from people and checked their DNA. They would then link those people to others who had any similar DNA records, ranking them in order of likely relationships. Depending on who else had submitted their samples, there was a possibility of finding links to my DNA from Mum's side of the family. It was a quite exciting prospect and, as Tim had pointed out, it did not depend on trawling through records of births, deaths, marriages, etc. to find links. I duly sent off for a DNA package and, when it arrived, dribbled into the sample tube. After posting the sample, it was now just a question of waiting for the results.

Tim had agreed to do the analysis of the DNA results when they arrived. Using the findings from his own DNA sample, he could hopefully eliminate those people who were on my Dad's side. That would leave the rest who would all be potential blood relatives of Mum. It would not be a simple task, but it might be the last hope we had of identifying Mum. A few weeks later, the results arrived. Before looking at the individual people linked to me, I looked at the ethnicity result which was quite interesting. It stated that my DNA ethnicity was made up of 72% England and Wales (mainly from Southern England/ Wales and West Midlands), 21% Ireland and Scotland (mainly Scotland) and 7% Norway. The Scandinavian bit was noted- maybe Mum was from Norway! The other results were not surprising. My grandmother on Dad's side, Kate Grindlay, was Scottish which would account for that result, but the lack of Irish

confirmed that Mum was not Marie Cremin. Dad was
from the London area and, so too, we suspect, was Mum,
hence the Southern England connection. I then moved on
to look at individuals. There was only one person in the
'extremely high' (Close Family) category and that was
Tim. Hardly surprising, but it did suggest that the DNA
linking process was working. The next category was also
'extremely high' (Second cousin) and there were three
matches: Steve Grindlay, Stephen Foster and Bill
Grindlay. It was obvious that the two Grindlay men must
be relatives of Kate Grindlay from my Dad's side of the
family. Stephen Foster, however, could be a relative of
Mum's. I checked the Cambridge Blues- no Foster. I
checked for a Helen Foster – no match! The results moved
on to Third cousins, Fourth cousins, etc. There were a lot
of matches and, as I found out later, the list would grow
as more people did the DNA test. I gave Tim access to my
results and waited for him to analyse them. In the
meantime, I looked at some of the family trees attached to
people in the list to see if I could spot anything. I also
messaged a few people, explaining the background to the
mystery of Mum's identity, in the hope that they may
know a Helen in their family. I had a few replies
expressing interest in my quest, but they were unable to
shed any further light on it.

Another feature of the results presented was the location
map and surnames that are common to both me and my
match. Using this, I was able to establish that Stephen
Foster was on my dad's side. I messaged Tim:

'George Draper Lovering appears on the Stephen Foster

family tree so I guess he is not the link to my Mum. I haven't looked on the tree, but it appeared as common to both trees when using the location map on DNA. Maybe not reliable to use that as Lovering does not appear on surname matches!'.

Tim had not seen this but checked it out. He responded:

'Ah, that means the location is shared, rather than the names. However, I do think in all likelihood he is a Lovering. His ancestor Henry George Foster (b. Hastings 1871) seems to pop out of nowhere when he joins the army in 1890. Leonard B Lovering's brother George Henry Lovering (b. Hastings 1871) disappears from the record at the same time. Henry Foster gives his father's details as an engineer named George, which is also a match. This is exactly the right generation to make Stephen your second cousin. So I think we may have inadvertently solved a different, minor mystery. (It was very common to use a false identity when joining the army). Probably interesting to Mr Foster, who should be called Lovering'

I messaged Stephen Foster to break the news to him that he was really a Lovering! Just this small revelation made me appreciate the possibilities of what we might find using these DNA results.

A couple of weeks later, Tim sent me a spreadsheet with his initial analysis of the results. He had colour coded the list to indicate which were definitely on the Lovering side and those which might be from Mum's family. Tim also indicated whether they were from my results or his results. During the next few months, I got updates from Tim on his progress. He also shared with me a new family tree he had constructed. He was quite confident that Mum's side of the family could be traced back to a couple from Aberdeenshire. They were James Robb and Ann Turner of Birse in Aberdeenshire who were both born in 1827. It would appear that many of their family moved to the USA which may rule them out as being Mum's ancestors. There were also many Smiths and Turners in the tree. Tim would have been happier if there had been more unusual names to follow. Naturally, I checked my Cambridge Blues list for all these surnames. I had messaged another of my matches and 'JeanDuncan 84' wrote; "I did have relatives that lived in Glasgow, Edinburgh, Penston and other places in the Lothians. Also had a grandmother who was born in Aberdeen as were her folks. I have met a 4th cousin in Musselburgh and have visited her several times. We have become great friends. My two Scottish families arrived in Utah in 1861, and 1868. We have kept in touch with the Edinburgh family ever since-well, at least until the one died. I also met a third cousin who lives in London on the Brown side of my family." This comment confirmed Tim's findings about the Aberdeen link and that I probably have many cousins living in the United States.

Tim continued to keep me up to date with his findings: For example,

'A small DNA update - I think I have narrowed down the likely ancestors on the one side to a particular couple, John Turner (b. 1784) and Isabel Smith (i.e. I've eliminated some of the earlier possibles on the "ABERDEENSHIRE" tree). Shame they are such common names'

Later,

'New ancestors John Bird and Susannah Tash of Great Cressingham, Norfolk, married 19 July 1790. Evidence for this is pretty good.
Almost certainly on your mum's side, although I guess their daughter Mary (b. 1799) could be Joseph Lovering's partner Mary Draper, as I believe that was not her maiden name (possibly why they didn't get married despite banns)'

And later, still,

'So far, the point where the two 'groups' intersect is the marriage of James Smith and Helen Jolly, so I am going to concentrate on working forward from this couple, and hopefully find someone who marries into the Tash family of Norfolk sometime between 1920 and 1925.
I already have one who migrated to the London area and married someone from Norfolk, but unfortunately a decade too late'

Tim also added two more family trees; one for the Bird family of Norfolk and another for the Perry family. I was grateful for Tim spending his time researching the problem, particularly as he was clearly an expert in genealogy and spotted things other people would miss. I was very optimistic that we might get some concrete results from his efforts.

I decided to visit Karen on what would have been Simon's sixty-second birthday. I did not want her to be on her own on such a significant date. We visited Simon's grave again and it was clear that his loss was still very raw for her ten months later. She somehow felt she could have done more for him that day he died. She also felt that the Health Service might have been able to diagnose his condition earlier and sorted something. I need not have worried about Karen being alone as that evening Stef, Simon's very good friend from the golf club, visited the house with his wife and, later, Karen's brother and his wife also arrived. It was a lovely evening spent talking about Simon and celebrating his life. I told everyone about the work that Tim had been doing with the DNA results and how I hoped it would solve the mystery of Mum. We talked about Dad and how he had moved to Malta before he died. Karen recalled the visit she made to Malta with Simon. They had managed to find Dad's death certificate and were able to visit the point nearest to where he was buried at sea. Karen also reminded me that they had information to suggest that Dad's widow, Claire, was still alive. Although the visit was a few years before, perhaps that was still the case. Karen suggested that maybe I should visit Malta and see if I could find her. Claire might even know something about Mum. I thought it unlikely she would be able to tell us much about Mum. After all, why would Dad want to talk about his previous love life? Of course, Claire might not want to have contact with us at all. The idea of a visit to Malta really appealed to me. Even if I could not trace Dad's widow, if she was still alive, then, at least, I could visit Dad's last resting place. I had never really known my Dad so it might give me some sort of connection with him.

When I got home, I put the idea of the visit to Pauline. Perhaps we could travel there during the Easter holidays and celebrate our wedding anniversary at the same time. However, we discovered that each of our Easter holiday dates were different, so we would have to go the week after our anniversary instead. Pauline liked to visit her Mum in Manchester as often as possible, so I suggested that we fly from Manchester. That would mean a very early morning flight. I contacted Colin to tell him of our plans and he said he was keen to join us, along with Corina, and would sort out the accommodation too. I was pleased that he wanted to come along too as it would give us a chance to spend some time together and 'visit' Dad.

I knew Dad's widow was called Claire. I was always saying, 'the internet is good!', so I decided to Google 'Claire Lovering Malta'. To my surprise, a result was found, but it was an obituary from The Malta Times. My heart sank. I clicked the link and read the obituary:

"FOSTER. On January 8, at Mater Dei Hospital, ANNABELLE SHIRLEY, aged 87. She leaves to mourn her loss her beloved sister Claire Lovering, her very dear god-daughter Eleanor Scerri and her devoted friend and helper Guido Said. A funeral service will be held on Thursday, January 12 at 10.30am at Holy Trinity church, Sliema."

It was an obituary, not for Dad's widow, but her sister. The funeral was at the start of that year so I knew that Dad's widow, Claire, was still alive ten months earlier. There was a good chance that we might find her when we visited Malta four months later. I then had an idea. I could try contacting the church where the funeral was held and see if they had any contact details for Claire. Again, the internet provided the tools to do that. There was no email contact for the church itself but there was for the Head of the diocese in Valletta, the capital of Malta. I sent an email explaining that I was the son of Claire's husband. I would be visiting Malta the following Easter and would be interested in making contact with her- if they knew of her whereabouts. I gave my contact details and asked them to forward the message to her if that was possible. Imagine my surprise when, within days, I got a response. The email had been forwarded to Claire and returned with the reply: 'I have spoken to Mrs Lovering and she accepted to meet Mr Rick Lovering when he comes to Malta. She will, in fact, write him a letter'.

I was thrilled by the response. Not only had I traced Claire but she appeared happy to have contact with me. I eagerly awaited the arrival of the letter. By a strange coincidence, the postman delivered it on my birthday, just as I had received the first contact with David a couple of years earlier. It was a wonderful birthday present. I opened the letter and read it.

"Dear Rick,

I was surprised and amazed to have your e-mail from the church - how clever of you to track me down and thank you for getting in touch. I knew Arthur had three sons but he never spoke of you to me – in fact I didn't know your first name till I got the e-mail and still don't know your brothers.

However, we kept in touch with Bob and I was

devastated to hear of his death 4 years ago. I was very fond of Bob and he and Jan used to visit us every year and we had some lovely holidays abroad together – happy memories! Tim and Juliet came over for Shirley's funeral and it was a great comfort to have them beside me.

I only wish I had known you and your brother but your Dad was very reticent and never spoke of you and I never liked to ask.

So now I have the chance to meet you when you come to Malta in April. I must keep going until then! I am 92 and confined to a wheelchair and I must get through the winter now. I expect you both have families and I look forward to hearing about them.

Sadly, your Dad suffered from many heart problems and we had to go to England for a heart valve replacement. This was only partially successful and he suffered a lot, so we lived quietly here in Malta for the last three years of his life till he died on the 6th July 1982. And was buried at sea as he wished. I was terribly upset and worn out with looking after him and it was months before I came to life again. I was lucky to have my mother and sister to help me through and Shirley and I were together until her death – and it was her obituary that enabled you to find me.

I now live in Villa Messina – a Home for the elderly Maltese, there are about 300 residents here and only six of us Brits! However I have a nice room with views over the garden and am very well looked after.

Sorry if this seems a long letter but I was delighted to hear from you and look forward to your visit in the Spring. Also sorry for my bad writing – my eyesight isn't as good as it was – but thankfully I'm not deaf nor do I suffer from dementia! (I think).

With very best wishes to you and your brother – how lucky I am to have two new step-sons.
>   With much love,
>   Claire"

I read the letter again and began to digest the details of its contents and what that meant. My first thought was that Claire sounded quite excited that I had managed to find her. I particularly enjoyed her comment about surviving the winter so that she will be able to meet us. I was saddened that she barely knew of the existence of the younger sons and did not know our names, especially in light of the most stunning part of the letter. Not only had Bob visited Dad in Malta, as we knew, but he and his family had continued to see Claire regularly, even after his death. I felt some satisfaction to have tracked down Claire via the obituary for her sister, but now I found that Tim and Juliet had actually attended the funeral! I had informed Tim that I had found Claire and, a day after I received the letter, Tim sent an email to explain why he had not told us about his contact with her. This is what he wrote:

"Around 1980/81 Bob tracked down Arthur in Malta and made arrangements to visit him. I believe we visited him twice in 1981 and 1982. Arthur swore Bob to keep the whole thing private, for reasons I have no direct knowledge of. At six or seven years old, therefore, I had to become part of keeping this confidence. When Arthur died that year, the promise was effectively set-in-stone by circumstance.

Bob decided to stay in contact with Claire and her sister,

and we visited Malta a number of times during the 1980s…. Bob stayed in touch with Claire until his death. …I have been on several visits to Malta on my own, as it is a country I like very much. Whenever I have been recently, I have also visited Claire.

….I've been increasingly uncomfortable with being unable to share my knowledge of Arthur's last years, limited though it is. On balance, my obligations to my dad were greater. I realise this is not a happy message but I'm glad to be able to share what I know.   Tim."

I was glad that Tim was honest and up front about the situation, and it must have been hard for him to write that message, knowing how closely we had been working on the family tree and DNA. Colin wrote a wonderful reply to Tim to assure him that we fully understood his position. Colin had often mentioned the phrase, 'Secrets and lies', when talking about our family and, here was another secret that had been uncovered. We often suspected that Bob knew much more than he would disclose to us. This latest sensation made me wonder if he knew more about Mum too. We will never know. Whilst it must had been incredibly difficult for Tim to keep quiet about the visits all those years, my main sadness and regrets lay with Simon and Claire. Simon had travelled to Malta with Karen and would have loved to have met Claire. He was denied that opportunity by all the secrecy and would never get that chance again. Equally, Claire had been denied the knowledge of the rest of the family and, if the letter I had just received was anything to go by, she would have wanted to have connected with us years before. I found it quite hard to understand that Bob had seen her on many occasions and not discussed Simon, Colin or me at all. I can partly understand Dad not wanting to talk about us with Claire but, once he had died, surely Bob could have been a little more open. I guess it highlighted the whole problem of keeping secrets and telling lies. Over time, it is very difficult to alter the status quo. The secrets remain secrets and the lies become the truth.

I wrote a reply to Claire immediately and included a potted biography of each of Arthur's six children to give her some idea of what we had done with our lives. I decided to write the letter using a word processor so it would be easier for her to read. That also meant that I was able to include some photos of the family. I also sent her the only photos I had of Dad. One was the photo of him with the three eldest children when they were young. The other was when he met royalty. I was always curious to know the story behind that. I posted the letter and, a week or so later, I received a reply. I, once again, opened the letter in anticipation of what I might find out about Dad and the family this time.

"Dear Rick,

Very many thanks for your letter and for sending photos and details of all the family. I had no idea that there were six of you and I was fascinated to read all the details of your lives. I am so grateful to you for taking so much trouble, especially on your birthday. I especially liked seeing most of you at your mother's funeral. She must have been an amazing person to bring up so many children so well.

As to the Princess Royal's visit to Cyprus, she did her best, but in spite of Arthur's explanations, she couldn't understand how the system worked. In those days all Army records were on punched cards as computers were only first coming into use. By the way, I expect that you knew Dad was officer in charge of all manpower statistics in the Near East (including Malta) as well as registering all civilian births, marriages and deaths.

When we got back to England, it was suggested that he should go to Worthy Down HQ to help with the transfer of punched cards onto computers. I am glad to say he refused! Later he finished his Army career by working as a Retired Officer for some years in the Ministry of Defence. So you are right to think your Dad's brains were inherited by you and Tom!

With kind regards to Pauline (sorry that my writing looks like a demented spider and hope that you can read this. Wish I could still type) With best wishes for your holiday – from Claire"

Claire was clearly pleased to find out about the 'new family' she had acquired. It was good to find out the story behind the photo of Dad with the Princess Royal which confirmed, also, that Dad and Claire were together in Cyprus.

The next letter I got came with a Christmas card and contained some bad news. Claire wrote:

"I am sorry not to have written sooner but I had a bad fall on Sunday. I was really in a mess with badly cut legs and bruised all over. I had to spend 2 days in hospital being patched up, x-ray, etc. I am back now in the home but still very shaky as you can from my writing!".

Her fall made us realise just how fragile she was. She was ninety-two years old after all. We were hoping she would avoid any further incidents before our visit three months later. Teasingly, she went on to write:

"I will write again after Christmas and tell you about Arthur's first marriage and the drama of how we met in Cyprus".

Those were two questions we would like to have answered, particularly about Dad's marriage to Marie Cremin. Perhaps, we would, at last, find out what happened to the real Marie. The story of how Claire met Dad in Cyprus suggested that Dad did not know Claire before he was posted in the Mediterranean. We always believed the family did not go to Cyprus with Dad because his relationship with Mum was over and he had another woman. That may have been true still, but the woman was not Claire. I was pleased to see that Claire would not be on her own over Christmas as some friends were visiting Malta to see her on Boxing Day. As for us, Pauline and I were due to meet up with Michael in New York and visit Tom. Christmas in New York was an exciting prospect.

The trip to New York was full of adventure but, unfortunately, I caught a virus of some sort and spent Christmas Day in my hotel room. That was after the start of the break was spoilt somewhat when we missed our connection at Dublin Airport and ended up flying into Newark Airport rather than JFK. The misery was compounded when my suitcase did not turn up. It appeared that my case did make the connection at Dublin, unlike us. I was not reunited with it until the early hours of the second night of our stay. I was still able to enjoy the holiday vibe in the Big Apple with the elaborately decorated shop displays and the Christmas tree at the Rockefeller, though it was bitterly cold. We went to see an American Football game at the New York Jets and a Christmas show at Radio City. When we returned to Bristol, both quite exhausted from the trip, I wrote another letter to Claire to tell her of our adventure across the Atlantic Ocean. I also mentioned that we were to spend the half term holiday in February in our favourite cottage on the Pembrokeshire coast, near St David's. It took a couple of weeks for me to recover fully from the virus that had struck me down in New York.

Claire replied quite promptly once again and, as I opened this letter, I was looking forward to hearing about Dad's marriage. I was to be disappointed as Claire made no mention of it. Perhaps she wanted to ensure I visited her by not telling me too much before then! Claire did describe the visit of her friends over Christmas and then remarked:

"I was sorry not have heard from Tim and Juliet and not even a card! I was upset about that as Shirley and I had done a lot to help Tim and paid school fees and helped him through university. However, I am so grateful that they came for Shirley's funeral otherwise I should have had no family to support me."

I could understand that Tim may have forgotten to send a card, given his present family situation with him working in Qatar and the rest of the family in Scotland. It was the statement about helping him through his education that stunned me. We had often wondered how Bob and Jan had been able to afford to pay Tim's school fees and the sacrifices they had to make. Well, it now seemed that they had a little help from Claire and her sister. Perhaps that was the true reason that Bob had asked Tim to keep quiet about the visits to Malta. A cynic might add that Bob kept news and information about the rest of the family from Claire, even after Dad's death, so that she would give more support to Tim. I do not like to think that Bob would be so mercenary, but the facts may suggest that he was. Claire went on to say:

"In your letter, you say that you are going to stay near St David's in February. Believe it or not, my dearest friend from our Aldbury days moved to Wales when Peter retired from Shell. He and Arthur were good friends and keen supporters of the British Legion. Catherine who is now 96 still lives alone (she sent me a lovely parcel of goodies at Christmas). She lives in Trefin a few miles from St David's and when I stayed with her, we used to go shopping and to church in the beautiful cathedral of St David's. I wondered if you would have time to call and see Catherine"

I thought 'It's a small world!'. For the first thirteen or fourteen years after having children, Pauline would drive the family down to a holiday cottage in Pembrokeshire, twice a year. At Easter, we headed for the south of the county and stayed at places such as Angle and Manorbier. In the October half-term holiday, we went to the north coast, usually to Porthgain or St David's. One year, we had booked a cottage in Trefin, the same small village where Claire's friend, Catherine, now lived. Who knows, Claire may have visited when we were there and said 'hello', as we passed each other on a walk along the Pembrokeshire Coast Path. Claire finished her letter by remarking that she had looked at our photos and could not see any resemblance with Arthur who she went on to describe as: "very slim, medium height and, in his last years, weighed only 8 stone compared to my 10 stone plus! He had a lovely head of thick white hair and a military moustache". It was great to read Claire's letters as I was now beginning to build up an impression of the father I never knew. I was yearning to hear more stories about him and, as always, tried to get my reply in the post as soon as possible. I also wanted to tell Claire that we would love to visit Catherine but felt it would not be right if two complete strangers turned up at her door, out of the blue. We had not even met Claire yet, so it seemed a little strange to drop in on her friends!

The morning of our journey to Pembrokeshire arrived and, shortly before we were due to leave home, the post arrived. There was a letter from Claire which started by telling us that Catherine had rung her and that she would be delighted to see us. That was good to hear. We could now call, knowing that she might be expecting us. The rest of the letter went on to reveal some more interesting facts about Dad and Claire. She wrote:

"I am always pleased to see the photos you send. Shirley and I had a disaster with our belongings which were packed in four crates which we had to leave here when they did lots of renovations to the Home. When we returned home, our boxes which should have been safely stored had been stolen or somehow disappeared. This was a tragedy for us as we lost all our photos, books and souvenirs from the past…". That was very sad to hear as I had hoped that Claire might have some photos of Dad for me to see. It would appear that might not be possible if she had lost them all in this incident. It seemed a little strange that family photos going missing was a recurring theme in the family. Bob had lost many of our photos in his move in Hereford, years previously. Some might consider there was a conspiracy of some sort! The letter went on to deliver a few more bombshells:

"You mention in your letter that your Dad visited you in Eastnor in 1964. What you did not know was that I was there too in the car waiting for Arthur! I went to keep him company on the long drive from Nottingham. I remember looking up the path to your house hoping someone would come out so I could see some of you and, of course, they didn't. When Arthur came out he (as usual) told me nothing except that he was going to stay with me which made me very happy. We were married on 14th May 1965 in London in a very quiet ceremony with just my family there which is what we wanted."

This really was astonishing news for me. To think that the last time I saw my Dad, and, perhaps, the only time I remember my Dad, Claire was there too. We had not yet met Claire but our paths had almost crossed on that day. Her story would confirm, just as we thought, that Dad's visit was to get Mum to agree to a divorce so that he could marry Claire. Since Mum was not really married to Dad so, technically, could not sign the papers, Dad would be a bigamist. She also mentioned travelling down from Nottingham so the story of Dad running a Wimpy restaurant in that city could also be true. Claire had already finished the letter, but then added another page which told of a truly remarkable part of Dad's life:

"To start at the beginning of your Dad's life. Did you know that at the age of about 6, he ran away from home because his stepmother was cruel to him. He lived rough in London for some time and was found by a friend of the family who took him in and then arranged for him to go to the Greenwich Naval School which had a boarding school for orphans or homeless children. When he left at the age of about 14, he was employed by Fyffes (the banana people) as a helper in the kitchen (galley I suppose) and travelled all over the world, South America, China, etc. When the War started, he joined the Army and served for many years."

Claire's letters were helping me to build a picture of my Dad and his life but this story took that to another level. It was hard to believe a boy of six running away from home and living rough in London. This would have happened just after the end of the First World War. I appreciate that times were different then, but it was still difficult to imagine one so young, living on the streets. Scenes from Charles Dickens' books came to mind. The other interesting thing about the story was the reason for his sadness, the cruel step-mother. I did not even know that my grandfather, Leonard Brasier Lovering, had married a second time. When we arrived at our cottage later that day, I went to the Ancestry UK website to find out who his second wife was. I discovered that her name was Ethel Lewis and that she and Leonard had two children, Violet and Joan. I could not trace any record of Violet getting married and having any children. Joan, however, married Frederick Kingston and they had a son, Geoffrey, born in 1948. Sadly, Geoffrey died in 2003. He was my half-cousin. As well as three brothers, I had now found out that Dad also had a half-sister. Leonard's first wife, my grandmother, Kate, did not die until 1923, according to previous research, which would mean that they must have got divorced when Arthur was a baby. My father had a quite traumatic early life, it would seem. I was aware, from Tim's article in the magazine on his military career, that he had been a merchant sailor and it was good to have a little more detail. He certainly got to see the world though working on a ship for Fyffes was bananas!

Our Pembrokeshire cottage was on the hillside overlooking Whitesands Bay, near St David's. In the distance, across the rather choppy waters, was Ramsey Island. At night, we could see the lighthouse, beyond Ramsey, flashing out a warning to sailors. It was very wild and windy on our first night there. I thought of Dad travelling around the world in his ship, full of bananas. It would not have been very pleasant being on the sea in the stormy weather that we were experiencing. I loved getting up early when we were staying at this cottage, so I could see the sun rise over St David's. Better still, however, was watching the sun set at the end of the day and we were treated to a beautiful scene that evening. The colours in the clouds and on the water were very special. The forecast for Monday looked quite promising, so we decided we would do the coast path walk from Trefin to Porthgain. We could visit Claire's friend, Catherine, and then have lunch at The Sloop Inn pub in Porthgain, before walking back to Trefin.

We drove up to Trefin and found somewhere to park in the village. Michael and his partner, Harriet, had come with us and we suggested that they started walking towards Porthgain and we would catch up with them. We intended to just visit Catherine briefly to introduce ourselves and say 'hello'. We found the cottage where she lived and there was an elderly man working in the front garden. We greeted him and explained who we were, before we glimpsed Catherine approaching the front door, which was already open. She looked quite sprightly for a ninety-six year old, although she took great care to walk around. She was delighted to see us and invited us in for coffee and biscuits. We declined the offer of refreshments, saying we would not stay for long. Catherine showed us into the front room and we began chatting. It was enthralling to hear her stories about how she met Claire and her sister. Apparently, she got to know Claire's sister at the Women's Institute in the village of Aldbury, where they all lived. Through her sister, Catherine got to know Claire and, of course, my Dad. We had already been in the house for some time when Catherine insisted that we have coffee and biscuits. She was also determined to sort the drinks herself, despite the steps and hazards in the kitchen. She was a truly remarkable person. We asked her to describe what my Dad was like. She said that was quite difficult to do though she did say he had a rather 'peppery' character! Catherine also told us about Pembrokeshire and how she adored it. We told her that we also loved to visit the county. She said, 'If you don't like wind, you won't like Pembrokeshire!'. It was certainly true that it was a windy place. She suggested that we try to get to St David's in May for the music festival, which she said was always interesting, and, if we did, we should try to visit her again. We had been with Catherine for well over an hour when we explained we would have to leave. Michael and Harriet would be waiting for us. Both Pauline and I had thoroughly enjoyed our time spent with Catherine. Pauline took a picture of me with Catherine that we would send to Claire. By the time we caught up with Michael and Harriet, they had already reached Porthgain. Michael was flying his drone over the harbour entrance to capture some stunning views on film. We got to The Sloop, only to find that food was not being served due to renovations. We made do with a packet of crisps as we, excitedly, told Michael and Harriet the stories that Catherine had told us. Michael suggested that, maybe, I had a bit of a 'peppery' character too! We used the term 'peppery' quite frequently after that day. I messaged Peta to tell her of the description of Dad. She replied to say that Dad had once snapped at Mum at a cocktail party, which suggested that he liked things to be done properly and would not tolerate slackness easily. The Pembrokeshire experience emphasised to me, the fact that I did not know my own father. Both Catherine and Peta could recall his mannerisms and character. Along with the stories that Claire had told me in her letters, I, at last, began to feel some sort of bond with him.

On our return from Pembrokeshire, I wrote to Claire to tell her of our meeting with Catherine and sent her the picture that Pauline had taken. It was only about a month until we were due to fly out to meet her for the first time, so we needed to make some arrangements. Claire told me that Andre, her helper, had booked a table at the Corinthia Hotel in Attard and that he would be able to drive her there. We would have lunch there with Andre and Claire, plus, of course, Colin and Corina. That would be on the Monday. Colin and Corina were returning to Romania the day after, so I told Claire that Pauline and I would also visit her on our own at her home in Rabat. Claire was pleased with the photo of me with Catherine. I was really looking forward to meeting Claire in Malta as I had grown very fond of her just through the letters that we had exchanged.

The Easter holidays arrived and Pauline drove us up to Manchester to stay at her mother's home. We had booked a taxi to collect us in the middle of the night to take us to Manchester Airport. We thought it would be quiet on an early Sunday morning, but the departure lounge was full of people. We landed at Luqa Airport in Malta at lunchtime and got a taxi to our hotel on the harbourside, near Sliema. Colin had organised the accommodation and he was at the hotel, with Corina, to greet us. He had, somehow, got a big room with a balcony and views over the harbour, because his courtesy car from the airport was late and he complained! Our room was next to theirs, rather smaller and with no views, except that of the buildings rising up on the slope of the hill behind the hotel. To be honest, we were happy just to be in Malta at last.

That evening, we went for a walk along the waterfront to a restaurant overlooking the harbour. We discussed the meeting with Claire which was to take place the following morning. She had mentioned the drama of Dad's first marriage in a letter, so we expected to find out a little more about Marie Cremin. Obviously, we would discover more about Dad, himself, and how he met Claire. It was very likely that we would not get the answer our main question: who was Mum? Would Claire know anything at all about her? After all, who would want to talk about their ex-lovers to their new love? At best, we might confirm that Mum's real name was Helen. The surroundings of the hotel might not make it easy for Claire to discuss her past freely. We agreed that we must play the situation by ear and be careful not to come across as the Spanish Inquisition. The main object of the day was to make Claire feel relaxed in our company and to get to know each other. Pauline and I would be visiting her a couple of days later at her home. We might have to wait until then to get the answers to our many questions.

Next morning, our taxi took us through the back streets of Gzira and headed for Attard, about a fifteen-minute drive from our hotel. Claire had recommended that we visit St Anton Gardens so we made our way there first.

The gardens were well maintained and full of colour. It was only a short walk from the gardens to The Corinthia Hotel. As we entered the lobby, Pauline spotted that Claire was already there waiting for us. As I approached her, I was greeted with a smile and she welcomed me as if we had known each other for years. This was our first ever meeting but, straight away, we all felt very relaxed. Andre, who was looking after Claire for the day and had just parked the car, appeared and offered to get us some drinks. Colin presented Claire with a few gifts from Romania. I gave her a small vase made of Bristol Blue glass. Andre then suggested we took our places at the table to have some lunch. Our planned strategy, of not pushing Claire too hard for stories of Dad, were quickly squashed as she was only too willing to talk openly about all sorts of things. She referred to the mystery of Mum's identity which rather bemused Andre, as he was obviously oblivious to the story. Colin explained to Andre about Dad marrying Marie Cremin and then Mum taking on her identity. His eyes widened with amazement as he heard about our search for the truth. I think he began to appreciate why we were so excited to finally meet Claire. He also realised that there was a mutual desire on part of everyone there to share information. Corina must have felt a little left out, but I noticed she was engrossed by all the tales as well. Pauline was sat next to Andre and, occasionally, got reassurance from him that Claire was coping well with the excitement of the day. We learned so much in those few hours that, at one point, Colin asked me if I was writing it all down. I said we'll just have to remember it later! I cannot recall the order in which Claire told us about her life with Dad, so I will just repeat them in chronological order.

Claire had mentioned in an earlier letter that she would tell me about Dad's marriage, so we listened eagerly as she told us the story. Naturally, she referred to Dad as Arthur.

"Arthur was away from home for several years during the Second World War, after being conscripted to join the army to fight in Italy and other places. On his return home, he approached the road where he lived, and suddenly realised that his house had been bombed!"

As I heard Claire tell me this, my immediate thought was that Marie had been killed in the bombing. 'So that's what happened to her', I thought, 'but, if Marie was dead, Mum would not have had to pretend that she was her. She and Dad could just have got married'.

Claire continued.

"Arthur thought that Marie had been killed, but some neighbours reassured him that she was all right and informed him of where she was now living. Arthur went to the address that he had been given and was shown into the room where Marie was waiting. On her lap, he saw a 'big, fat baby'! It was clearly Marie's child. At that moment, a man entered the room. Arthur pointed towards Marie and exclaimed 'That's my wife!'. The other man replied, 'She may well be your wife but she's my woman now!'. Arthur was so upset that he stormed out of the house, re-enlisted with the army and requested that he was posted as far away as possible! He was to spend the next two years in Burma"

There was a brief silence around the table. We were all astounded to hear that Marie had given birth to a child by another man whilst Dad was away. I tried to process what this meant. My theory that Arthur and Marie did not have any children because, maybe, Marie was unable to conceive, was clearly incorrect. There was certainly nothing wrong with Dad's ability to procreate having fathered at least six children. Why did they not have any children together as the electoral records certainly suggested that they were living together throughout the time from their marriage in 1932 until the War? Dad may have been away at sea some of the time, I suppose. The other thought I had, was thinking back to why Mum had taken Marie's identity? Marie was still alive so there was always a risk that she could turn up again at any time. How would Dad explain that to his colleagues as he had probably told them that Mum was Marie, even though, it was likely everyone knew her as Helen? It could have been very embarrassing for Dad to explain.

As promised, Claire told us the drama of how she met Dad. She ran a small tearoom, near Southwell Minster in Nottinghamshire. Claire got a little bored with life in the tearoom and decided to seek something more adventurous. The Women's Volunteer Service were looking for more mature women (over thirty years old) to join up and Claire saw this as an opportunity to have some adventure and see the World. She hoped to be posted in the Far East somewhere but ended up in Cyprus. The women on the camp, where she was posted, were billeted in a few huts. One night, there was a terrific storm and the roof was blown off Claire's hut. Arthur, my Dad, was the duty officer that night and he was responsible for ensuring that the women were found alternative accommodation. Arthur made sure that Claire got the best accommodation available. He had, obviously, noticed Claire before and this was his chance to get to know her. Claire had also had her eye on Arthur. This story illustrates just how relaxed Claire was, in telling us about Dad. After all, at that time, Dad was still 'married' to Mum, in that he still had Mum and the family back home in England. Claire was now telling this story to two of the young children who were deserted by their father all those years ago. The incident also confirmed again that Dad and Claire did not meet until after Dad had gone to Cyprus. We had thought that he wanted the family to stay in England as he already had another mistress. Maybe, he did, and Claire was the next one – the final one?

When Dad and Claire returned to England, Dad left the Army and set up a catering business. Claire explained that he invested in a Wimpy Restaurant franchise in Nottingham. We had now found out about that photo I remembered from my childhood: the one of Dad and a famous actress, opening a Wimpy in Nottingham. Claire went on to tell us that Dad employed a girl to manage the day-to-day business of running the restaurant and thought she was doing well. However, he discovered that quite the opposite was true. The venture was a disaster and Dad lost a lot of money. Claire and Dad then moved to the south coast and ran a café on the seafront at St Leonards in Sussex. Unfortunately, it was another business decision that was to backfire. Dad had not factored in that, during the winter months, few people went on the seafront. They tended to remain in the town centre instead. By this time, Dad had got a job with the Ministry of Defence as a Retired Officer and was making a daily commute to London. The problems in the café increased when the chef decided she could not work in the evenings. That meant that when Dad got home from work in London, he went straight back to work, cooking in the café. The business disasters effectively bankrupted Dad. I had not appreciated that Dad had even been in the catering business, but I suppose his work in the galley on the banana boat might have led him down this route. It was interesting that his eldest son, David, also went into the catering business too after leaving college.

It must have been around this time that Dad made that journey to Eastnor, with Claire, to finally tell Mum that their relationship was over for good. In reality, I suspect it was over many years before that. Now we always thought that Dad had made that visit to get Mum to sign the divorce papers, but it turned out, that was not the case. Claire went on to tell us another remarkable tale in the life of Arthur and herself. They both wanted to get married, but Claire told us that Arthur informed her that was impossible. He was already married to Marie, the real Marie, and he did not know where she was so he could not get a divorce. This exploded another myth about Dad. We thought there was a possibility that he was a bigamist. It turned out that he was a very honourable man and knew that pretending Mum was his wife would be fraudulent. Yet, on all our birth certificates, that is exactly the lie that he and Mum had lived with all that time. Perhaps, it said something about the love he had for Claire, that the lie had to end. Claire and Dad thought their hopes of being married were dashed until, a few weeks later, Dad received a letter addressed to Sergeant Lovering. He thought that was strange as, by then, he had left the Army as Lieutenant Colonel Lovering. He opened the letter and, to his surprise, discovered that it was from Marie! She had remembered that he did business with Lloyds Bank and, through the bank, had managed to track down his location. This was about twenty years after Arthur had last seen Marie, with her baby and new man. In the letter, Marie explained that she wished to re-marry but, of course, needed to get divorced from Arthur first. This was an astonishing coincidence which meant that both Arthur and Marie could fulfil their wishes: get divorced and then marry their new loves.

As well as telling us about her life with Arthur, Claire was equally keen to hear our stories about the family. There were several occasions when she said what a remarkable woman Mum must have been. I found it quite touching that she had such a healthy respect for Mum. There was also sadness, and a little frustration, that she had not got to know us earlier and, in particular, that she was not able to meet Simon. The time flew past and soon it was time for us to leave. Andre drove Claire back to her home in Rabat and we got a taxi to the hotel in Sliema. That evening, we went over the stories again. This time I made notes and pondered on all the things we had found out about Dad. As expected, Claire was not able to give us any more information about Mum. It had been a truly wonderful afternoon and one I would certainly never forget.

Colin and Corina flew back to Romania in the early hours of the following day. Pauline and I had a day in Valletta before returning to the hotel. We had decided that, in the evening, we would walk up to St Julian's so we could see Dragonara Point. Dad was buried at sea, a few miles off the cliff at Dragonara Point. We had found that Claire's old church was on the way, so we visited that as well. We discovered that we could see the tower of the church from our hotel window! When we reached St Julian's, I noticed that Pauline moved away a little and left me alone with my thoughts. It was quite strange to look out to sea, beyond the tip of Dragonara, and to think that was where Dad was laid to rest. I had not really known Dad when I was little, so it was quite moving to be re-united with him again in a spiritual way. This trip to Malta had brought me closer to him in many ways.

Wednesday was to be our last day in Malta and we had arranged for a taxi to take us to Claire's home in St Dominic's Square in Rabat. The building looked very impressive from the outside but, once we were inside, it felt more like a hospital institution. We signed in and were given directions to Claire's room. We walked along a corridor which was full of old people, sitting expressionless, in their chairs and wheelchairs. It was quite a depressing place. We knocked on the door and Claire greeted us. She apologised to us that she was not able to offer us a cup of tea. The residents were not permitted to have a kettle in their rooms. They were also not allowed to have pets, but there was a cage in Claire's room containing two finches. It was good that she had some company. Claire explained that she had quite a large room as it was the one that she used to share with her sister, Shirley. They had allowed Claire to keep the room for just herself. Pauline had brought a pew sheet from the Anglican Cathedral in Valletta that she had visited the day before. She and Claire had a long conversation about each other's work in their churches. Claire was no longer able to attend services at her church but a priest did visit her to offer communion. She was pleased that we had visited her church in Sliema.

We also talked extensively about the family again. We found out that Bob had visited Malta just a matter of days before Dad died. I had not realised that he saw Dad so soon before his death. That would explain how Mum was able to tell me that the World Cup finished him off. It was the World Cup where Northern Ireland had much success and, apparently, Dad leapt up when the Irish scored a goal in one game. It appeared that Dad's love of Irish things lasted right up till the end! Claire commented that she had found Colin an interesting character. She also commented that Dad had once said to her that he thought that Colin might not be his child! This was quite astonishing, though not entirely a surprise. Perhaps the story of the wrong baby being brought back from the hospital had an element of truth after all. It was the cover story for Colin having a different father to the rest of us. Simon always commented on Colin's ginger hair. Was Colin the Prince Harry of the family?

One of the staff brought Claire's lunch into the room. It was time for us to leave. Claire said she would try not to cry but we felt quite emotional too as we closed the door behind us. Although Andre visited Claire with his young family occasionally, she was basically on her own again. Pauline said it was important that we gave her something to look forward to. When I got back to Bristol the next day, I booked another flight out to Malta for three months later.

I was due to visit Colin in Bucharest a few weeks after our trip to Malta. Tim had told me before that his task of trying to find Mum using Ancestry DNA would be made easier if more of the family submitted samples. Following Claire's comment about Dad doubting he was Colin's father, I felt it was essential that Colin sent a sample, so we could find out the truth. I ordered a pack for him and took it with me to Romania. I only stayed in Bucharest for a few days, but it gave me the opportunity to have some really honest conversations with Colin about our lives and also about writing this book about Mum and Dad. It made me realise that we did not always make the time to talk to each other in our busy lives. Maybe, if I had talked to Mum a little more, I would not be writing this now! I posted Colin's sample when I got home. Now we just had to wait for the results.

We sent a photo of our visit to Claire to Catherine in Pembrokeshire. She was really pleased to receive it and wrote back to thank us. She also informed us that the line-up for St David's Festival was not very good this year. Claire and I continued to exchange letters and I learned a few more details of her life. She ran various WVS clubs and other bars in Berlin which was rather enlightening. Pauline was also correct about giving her things to look forward to as she had already planned another lunch for my return to Malta three months later. Claire also recounted another story from her time in Cyprus which gave me a glimpse of another side of Dad's character:

"..your Dad and I were invited to a weekend at the General's Ski-ing Lodge in the Troudos Mountains (no snow at the time there). I was very nervous and wondering what I should wear, etc. However, the General was very welcoming and a good host. I was very apprehensive though as I had heard that after dinner, they always played strip poker. However, all went well as they first played ordinary poker but I just had to watch as I didn't know how to play.

"Arthur really enjoyed himself as he knew all of the other guests. I felt rather left out of things and went to bed feeling rather miserable and very cold (that mountain air). Later my bedroom door opened and Arthur slipped in (thank goodness he found the right room!). I was so pleased to see him and was very soon nicely warmed up."

Claire also commented on my keenness to cycle everywhere and then told me that, soon after the War, she and Shirley cycled across France! She certainly had led a very interesting life.

I got a Facebook message from Tim. Colin's DNA results were now available. I went on to Ancestry to have a look at my matches and there was Colin, at the top of the list, as expected. I checked to see the shared matches – those people who shared DNA with both me and Colin. They included the Grindlay people. It meant that Dad was wrong. Colin was his child. We had brought the right baby back from the hospital. Colin was a Lovering!

9 MARIE

After returning from Malta, I decided to upgrade the subscription that I had with Ancestry UK. I had previously had access only to the UK records provided by the service. Now I would be able to search records worldwide. My thinking was that Mum was possibly born overseas and thus any search for her would be fruitless on the old subscription. Whenever I had some time to kill, I would do searches on the website to see what came up. These searches were often linked to names that Tim had put on the 'Mum' family trees. Tim was continuing to use the matches from our DNA results to build family trees that link those matches that are not on Dad's side of the family. I would still cross reference these with the Cambridge Blues list and search for Hilda Audrey too (the name Mum used on Peta's birth certificate).

I don't know if it was a coincidence or not, but, soon after the upgrade, I was looking at tips on the Ancestry website relating to Dad. I noticed there were some photos attached to Arthur Walter Lovering. When I opened them, I discovered many had been posted by Tim the previous

Summer. I had not come across these before and was a little surprised that I had missed them. There were many photos that I had never seen before, including a lovely one of David, Bob and Peta when they were young. Also, amongst the photos, were some pictures taken on Bob's visits to see Dad and Claire in Malta. Although the quality of the photos was not great, it was exciting to see more images of my father in his last years. I contacted Tim to ask him about the pictures and whether he had any more. He replied that he did not. I also suggested that he send copies to Claire, as she no longer had many of Dad following the disaster of losing her boxes of photos and documents. Tim said that he would do that. It had been a joyful experience seeing these 'new' photos and made me wonder if there were more somewhere, to be discovered. I would love to have seen a picture of Mum when she was younger or one of her and Dad together.

There were also some pictures of documents amongst Tim's attachments to Dad on the Ancestry site. There was an extract from The Times, announcing the wedding of Dad to Claire in 1965. It included the address of Claire's parents' house in Nottinghamshire. Out of curiosity, I looked up the property on the internet, just to see what Claire's family home looked like. It was a rather grand house which was several centuries old. It would suggest that Claire's parents were quite well off although, of course, if you saw a picture of Cryalls House in Kent, where we lived, you might think that we were quite wealthy too! There was a clip from The London Gazette dated May 1963. In it, The War Office listed those officers that were leaving the Army and Dad was included. On another extract from The London Gazette newspaper, dated 9th April 1970, there was a list of companies that were no longer solvent. Included in the list was 'A W Lovering (Caterers) Limited'. I assumed that was the company name that Dad used when running the Wimpy Restaurant in Nottingham and the café on the seafront at St Leonards, near Hastings. Claire had told us that he had been bankrupted and there it was, in black and white, in the newspaper. All these documents were attached to Dad on Tim's family tree for the Lovering family (separate to his 'Mum' trees from DNA). I didn't recall seeing the tree before and looked forward to studying it in more detail another time. However, the next time I looked for it, the tree was not there anymore. Tim had changed the settings to make it 'private'. This was a common setting for users of Ancestry who did not wish for the general public to have access to the details on their tree. The reason that I had not come across the pictures of Dad before was probably because Tim always had his tree set on 'private' and may have, by mistake, made it public briefly. I was grateful that I had, by chance, stumbled across those pictures and documents which gave me just a little more insight into Dad's life.

I often got frustrated with the search engine used by Ancestry UK. It seemed to pick some of the results at random and some did not even match the search criteria. If I said someone lived in London, I still got results for the United States. Even the gender was often different. For some searches, I knew there were good matches, but they did not appear in the results. This particularly occurred when looking at details of close family. The randomness of the results of the searches were quite baffling. One evening, I decided to search in Births, Deaths and Marriages for 'Marie Lovering'. I had certainly tried this before but, this time, I got quite surprising results. There was a record of a Marie Lovering getting married to Walter J. Murray in Bournemouth at the end of 1969. Could it be that I had found the second marriage of Marie Cremin? Claire had told us that Dad had received a letter from Marie, asking for a divorce, when Dad and Claire wanted to get married. Dad remarried in 1965 so I would have expected Marie to get married soon after then, but this marriage was four years later. Maybe it wasn't her after all, although I vaguely remembered Claire mentioning that Marie had moved to the south coast. Bournemouth is on the south coast. I made another search on Ancestry to see if there were any results for Marie Murray, the new married name of Marie Cremin. I was in luck. A result showed that Marie Murray died in June 1978 in Bournemouth. That must be the same person, I decided. The record also gave Marie Murray's date of birth. It was given as 11th December 1910. I checked the birth certificate of Marie Cremin. The birthdates matched! I had, at last, found out what happened to Marie Cremin. I messaged Colin in Romania to tell him the news. His response made me realise, once again, the strange circumstances of my Mum and Dad. He said, 'it was strange to think it was her name that appeared on all our birth certificates'. He was right. This woman who married Walter in 1968 was probably completely unaware that, officially, she was the mother of six children! I very much doubt that Dad would have informed her of all his children. He would have been just happy to have finally got the divorce from her when he had contact with her in 1964 or 1965. Another thought crossed my mind. Bob was, briefly, at Bournemouth College of Technology in the late sixties. Bob and Marie could well have passed each other on the street!

The next day, I looked at the marriage certificate of Arthur Walter Lovering to Marie Cremin from 1932. The marriage that had led to Marie's name being on our certificates and the marriage we thought was to our Mum, until we found out the truth in 1982. They were married in the Church of Our Lady of Victories in Kensington. It occurred to me that I had never visited the church. I looked it up on the internet. The church was Roman Catholic and stood in Kensington High Street. Unfortunately, the church was destroyed by a bomb during the Second World War and was then re-built again in peacetime. I was due to go to London for a concert and I intended to visit David as well that day. It was just a short tube ride from Paddington Station to Kensington High Street, so I decided I would pay a visit to the church. On the day, it was quite easy to find the church and, after briefly admiring the building, I went inside. This was not the same building that witnessed the marriage of Arthur and Marie, but I felt their spirit there, nonetheless. I had stood outside their house at the time of their marriage, about thirty years earlier, and now I was at the spot where the ceremony had taken place. It felt quite a special moment and I thought about what happened to them afterwards. Marie died in Bournemouth, forty-six years later, and Dad passed away in Malta just four years after her. I posted a picture of the church on the Lovering page on Facebook. Colin remarked about the sign outside the church stating the times for 'confessions'. They both had much to confess!

After leaving the church, I got the tube to St Pancras and then caught the train to Ashford in Kent. It was good to see David again and, this time, I was able to stay longer and have a good chat about the visit to Malta and what I had found out. I gave him a copy of the photo of him, with Bob and Peta, that I had found on Tim's tree on Ancestry. I asked him if he had any further memories of Mum and Dad when he was young. He explained that, because he was at boarding school for much of his early life, he never really spent a lot of time with his parents. He repeated the story of going on holiday with Dad, when Mum remained at home looking after the youngest children or was pregnant again. We discussed what progress had been made on trying to find out who Mum really was. I suggested that there may be a link with our Godparents and, also, possibly, the Lenham family who visited us in Ledbury in the 1970s. David did not know who his Godparents were though he did think that he was named after a Scottish explorer called Ian. David's middle name is Ian. This got me quite excited. Tim had found a strong Scottish link in his research using the DNA matches. Could it be that this Scottish explorer, Ian, is somehow related to Mum, maybe even her father? Being an explorer might fit with her stories of travels around the World. Mixing with the Maori tribes in New Zealand. Staying at the Convent School in Belgium whilst her Dad traversed the deserts and jungles of the World. David was very sceptical whether any of Mum's stories were based on any truth at all, anyway. As I said goodbye to David and left to catch my train to London, I realised that I had just had the longest conversation ever with him, yet he is my brother and we are both over sixty years old. All those years of David being estranged was the reason why. It also reminded me that I should have had similar conversations with Mum whilst she was still alive then, maybe, I would not be still seeking answers about her, over ten years after her death! When I got home, I Googled for 'Scottish explorer Ian'. The only person I could find who might fit the description was not an explorer, as such, but John (Ian) Bartholomew, who had inherited and ran the famous mapmaking publishing company. His birthdate of 1890 was about right for having a daughter in the 1920s and, surely, a map publisher would entail trips around the World. It might also explain my personal passion for maps. When growing up, I would, often, much prefer to read an atlas than a book! It was an intriguing thought but neither of my cross checks would suggest that he was Mum's father. There were no Bartholomews in the list of Cambridge Blues or in any of the families that Tim had linked to us using the DNA results.

I had picked up a few facts or stories from conversations with members of the family, so I always raised the issue of Mum's identity, whenever we met up, in the hope that they might recall some new useful piece of information. I visited Colin's son, Dan, in Ledbury when Colin was over from Romania to see his grandson, Fred. When talking about his gran, Dan was reminded of the occasion when he had a project to do for school. He interviewed Mum about her experiences during the Second World War.

Unfortunately, he had no recollection of what she said in the interview, nor had he kept anything like that from his school days. I would love to know the stories that she told Dan as they may give a clue as to where she came from and, perhaps, how she eventually met Dad. Did she repeat the stories she had told us about working at Fighter Command in the Operations Room or was that just a fantasy she told us after watching a war film? A week, or so, later, I was standing on the beach by the donkey rides at Weston-super-Mare. It was the Weston Air Day and Claudette, my niece, was there with her husband, Andy, as a weekend treat for her birthday. There was an hour to wait before the flying would commence, with a display by an RAF Typhoon. We got chatting about the mystery of Mum. Andy was new to the family, so I was able to give him the background to the Lovering story and what we knew about Mum. Claudette then remembered that she had been watching a film about Russia with Granny (Mum) and Claudette told her that she would like to live in Russia. Granny replied that that was interesting as she once lived in Russia! What's more, Granny claimed that she could speak Russian too. I had not heard this story before and it added to the theory that, maybe, Mum had travelled quite extensively before she met Dad. Either that, or her brain was coming up with even more fanciful stories.

My second trip to Malta to visit Claire was fast approaching and I received a letter from her which gave details of where we would meet for lunch this time; at a rather posh hotel in Naxxar. In the letter, Claire also recounted a story that Dad had told her, of his wartime adventures in Italy. She wrote:

"I do know that he started the War in Egypt, was commissioned in Palestine. Does the word SALERNO mean anything to you? It is about 20-30 miles south of Rome and there was a mini-invasion there and Arthur was stranded there for several months living in trenches and firing their heavy guns at the Germans till finally they were evacuated and the invasion was called off. Your Dad was second-in command there and the Commanding Officer was George Sheen (?) and after that they spent a cold and miserable winter in a railway tunnel above Florence. I don't remember much else except that they fought their way up to Lake Garda"

I had heard of Salerno but did not know much about it. I vaguely recalled there being a bit of a mutiny in the British Army. I hoped that Dad was not involved in the mutiny. I looked for information on the internet and discovered the whole operation seemed to be a military mess. I decided to order a book about the landings on the beaches of Salerno to find out more. When the book arrived, I noticed that the appendix listed the regiments involved in the campaign. I checked, from Tim's article on Dad's military history, which regiment Dad was in. It was not included in the book! Was Dad really at Salerno, or was it another fantasy tale from my parents? I felt I needed to get hold of Dad's military service records, so I could check that Tim's facts were correct. I discovered that I could obtain a detailed record of his military service if I got permission from his next of kin. That was Claire in Malta, and I would be visiting her soon, so I could ask her to sign the form giving me permission. In the meantime, I looked up Dad's regiment on the internet and found there was a site where family or ex-army personnel posted their memories of the regiment and included some photos too. I scrolled through the photographs, looking to see if there were any of Dad. I came across one which included a man surrounded by four men who were not wearing their shirts. The man was smiling and reminded me a little of Bob. Could this be Dad? This particular man was dressed slightly smarter than those around him. I believed Dad would have been a sergeant, possibly, by then, so would have rank over the other men, hence, he was keeping up appearances, maybe. I made a copy of the picture so I could show Claire. Perhaps, she would be able to tell me if it was really Dad. I felt quite excited that I might, at last, have an image of Dad during his army days in Italy.

It was strange flying into Malta again in early July. Just a few months previously, the island meant little to me. It was the place where my Dad lived his final years. Now, as I looked out the window of the aircraft, I could see Mdina below and tried, without success, to spot St Dominic's Monastery which is next to Claire's home. I was travelling alone this time, as Pauline had to go to work. I was nearing retirement and only worked one day a week. The last trip to Malta, at Easter, had been really exciting and we found out much about my Dad's life. I wondered whether I would learn anything new this time. It would be good to see Claire again as she had many stories to tell. I was staying at the same hotel in Gzira as before. On my first evening, I decided I would walk towards St Julian's and Dragonara Point, so I could see where Dad was laid to rest again. It was a Sunday evening and the prom around Ballutta Bay was busy with tourists and locals enjoying the warm sunshine. I was interested to see several water polo matches taking place in the pools fenced off in the sea. I had never seen water polo live before and stood and watched for several minutes. I continued my walk and found a spot where people were sunbathing on the flat, worn rocks by the water. I made my way carefully towards the water's edge and filled a small plastic bottle with some sea water. I had promised Karen, Simon's widow, that I would do this and then, when I returned to Simon's grave in Worcester, I would pour the water on the grave. It sounds a little silly, but it was my way of reuniting Simon with his father. You never know, there might be a molecule of Dad's body in that bottle!

The 2018 World Cup tournament was in progress and I noticed that most of the restaurants and bars had televisions on, showing the latest match. I was getting hungry, so I found a restaurant that overlooked the sea. In fact, I could see Dragonara Point in the distance from my table. It was a few miles off the Point that Dad was buried at sea. I ordered my food and checked my bottle of Mediterranean water was all right. The round of 16 game between Spain and the hosts of the World Cup, Russia, was nearing its end. The game was level at 1-1 and a small group of Spanish fans, on a nearby table, were looking rather anxious. The game went into extra time and then to penalties. I was loving the tension of penalties in the restaurant, especially as the Spanish fans could not believe it when they lost! It then occurred to me that I was close to where Dad ended his days and I was told that it was the World Cup that precipitated his death. He had got very excited when Northern Ireland scored a famous victory and he had leapt out of his chair, despite poor health. The team Northern Ireland defeated was Spain.

I met Claire for lunch at the Pallazo Pariso gardens the next morning. Andre joined us once again and I asked him to check the document regarding my request for Dad's military record before getting Claire to sign it. I gave Claire a copy of Tim's article about Dad's military career that had been published in the genealogy magazine about ten years previously. She did not remember seeing it before so was really interested to read it. I also presented her with a book of old pictures of Southwell, the town in Nottinghamshire where she grew up. Surprisingly, most of the talk over lunch was about the World Cup. I told Claire about watching the Spain versus Russia match and learned that she had been watching some of the World Cup matches too, though she confessed she was not a huge football fan. I think she enjoyed hearing me recount the story of the 1970 Quarter Final game between England and West Germany which ended with Bob throwing a teapot at Simon, and breaking it, after he changed his allegiances to the Germans when they took the lead. Claire had also told me, in an earlier letter, about her memories of what happened when England won the World Cup in 1966:

'I was happy in my little shop selling bread and homemade cakes- but Arthur was depressed and miserable with nothing to do. Then we had the brilliant idea that we would do some outside catering. Arthur enjoyed cooking and I had a lot of experience catering. The result was good and we were booked to cater for a wedding reception for about 50 people in the next village hall. We then realised it was the Saturday of the World Cup Final. Of course, we had to go ahead and ordered an extra large television to put on the wall so that all the guests could see the match. After the church service, everyone rushed into the hall and were joined by the other villagers who wanted to see the match on the big TV. Chaos ensued and my tasteful buffet was untouched! Grannies and children disappeared and we were left with a seething mass of men (and a few women) who were only interested in the match and the drinks (poor bride). Actually we found the match very exciting and what a celebration we had. What wasn't good was clearing up afterwards- a mammoth task. This was more or less the end of our career in catering and we finally decided that we were too old for it!'

I had a day of sight-seeing around Valletta and getting the ferry over to the three cities before a rather nervous evening, watching England scrape into the Quarter Final of the World Cup on penalties. The next morning, I caught two buses to get me from Gzira to Rabat. It was very early in the morning when I got there so I spent half an hour wandering round the 'silent city', Mdina. It really was silent as there were no tourists about, except me. A wonderful experience. I then made my way through the streets of Rabat to Claire's residence in Villa Messina. Claire greeted me when I knocked on her door. We talked briefly about the football before Claire showed me some of the pictures in the book that I had given her. One showed the pub which was next door to her sister's house. Shirley's cat used to spend much time in the pub! Claire then turned to a picture of a rather grand house which featured two tennis courts on the front lawn. Claire informed me that this was her childhood home, Normanton Hall, though there was only one tennis court when she was there! This led to a discussion about her parents and I got the impression that Claire did not get on particularly well with her father. Her father was a solicitor and her sister, Shirley, also trained to become a solicitor. Claire felt that her sister was her Dad's favourite and she was quite pleased to get away from the family when she took up voluntary work overseas with the Women's Voluntary Service.

We talked about Mum. I was hoping that, maybe, Claire might recall another snippet of information which would help in my quest to identify her. I suggested that I thought that Dad probably met Mum when out one evening and then got her pregnant. To avoid the social embarrassment, he probably told her to pretend to be his wife, Marie. Claire said that she thought that Mum was working in a bar when she met Dad. This was news to me but confirmed my suspicions about how they got together. Claire then shocked me with another fact. She told me that Dad had also got her pregnant! It was before they had got married so her parents were not at all pleased about the situation. Claire was in her late 30s by then and, sadly, the pregnancy failed at an early stage. I commented that pregnancies before marriage seemed to feature quite regularly in the Lovering family and that it seemed strange that Dad and Marie never had any children. Claire mentioned that Dad was very upset when Peta got pregnant before she married Steve. He couldn't understand how it happened as she was 'such a lovely girl'. I thought that a bit rich coming from a man who had got Mum pregnant (seven times?) out of wedlock and then Claire as well.

I showed Claire the photo of the man in Dad's regiment that I had come across on the internet. She said that it did look a little like Dad, but she thought it was not him. That was a little disappointing for me as I had hoped she would definitely identify him. Oh well, I would still keep it and suggest that it might be him. We discussed Dad's exploits during the War and Claire recalled that Dad had written down tales of his life in the Army. It focussed on what he had experienced with his fellow soldiers. It was quite a hefty piece of work and, when Dad and Claire moved houses, Dad decided it was too bulky to take with them. He offered it to Tim but, at the time, Tim wasn't interested in it. I could not believe what I was hearing. I had just bought a book about Salerno to try to find out a bit of what Dad went through in the War and now I find he had written his own account. I would love to have read that. Two of my nephews, Dan, with Mum's account and Tim, given the chance to hear Dad's story, had both not got the documents today. Together they would tell me a huge amount about both Mum and Dad. More documents to add to the list that had been lost or gone missing over the years.

Since I had my iPad on me, Claire and I spent some time looking through the old photos that I had. I came across one of our old flat behind the Market House in Ledbury that we lived in from 1969 until 1973. I had sent Claire a picture of the Market House in a recent letter, so I just reminded her about it. I was astonished to hear her tell me that she knew Ledbury quite well. She often stayed there with her sister, Shirley, when they visited Bob in Hereford. It had not occurred to me that the meetings between Bob's family and Claire were not just in Malta. Claire would have been in Ledbury in the years after Dad died. On the photo of Ledbury, I was able to explain to Claire how close it was to where Mum and I lived, and also to Peta's house. I felt sad again that we could have passed each other on the street in Ledbury and she would've had no idea that I was Bob's brother. She barely knew of my existence then and it was now thirty years later that we were talking about Ledbury!

The next thing she told me was even more staggering. Claire informed me that Shirley had helped to buy Bob's house in Hereford for him and he then paid rent to Shirley. Apparently, he had run into financial difficulties and was not always able to pay the rent. Many of the Lovering family got into trouble over money so I guess I was not totally surprised to hear that Bob had struggled with his finances too. His part dependency on Shirley's generosity might be another reason that he told Tim not to tell us about Claire and Shirley in Malta. It would also explain why he never told them anything about the rest of us. A combination of being a little embarrassed about the situation as well as making sure that he and his family were the only ones to benefit.

Before I left, I noticed a picture of Dad and Claire, with their dog, on her bedside table. It was a lovely photo of them and the best one that I had seen of Dad. I took out my camera and took a picture of it for myself. It was sad to say goodbye to Claire again and I promised that it would not be long before I returned and that I would bring Pauline again next time. I had been chatting with her for over three hours and had found it another joyful experience as we tried to fill in a few gaps for each other about our lives.

Several weeks after returning from Malta, I finally received the details of Dad's military service that I had requested. Strangely, the documents arrived on Claire's ninety-third birthday. The first page I saw was the form completed when Dad first left the service of the Territorial Army in 1944. The address of his wife, Marie, was given as Bessborough Road, Harrow whilst Dad's address was Woodland Road in Harrow. I assume that Marie's address was where Dad first encountered her on his return from fighting, when he was confronted with a big, bouncing baby on Marie's lap. The Bessborough Road address, however, had been crossed out and replaced with an address in Abbey Road in Torquay. This was hugely significant to me. Over thirty years previously, Pauline and I had travelled down to London to look for birth and marriage certificates at Catherine House. We had found the birth of Robert Andrew Lovering in Torquay in 1947 and his mother was listed as Marion Lovering, formerly Cremin. No father was named. We had always wondered whether Marion was, in fact, Marie as the similarities seemed too much of a coincidence. The Torquay address on Dad's discharge form seemed to confirm that Robert's mother was, indeed, the same woman that Dad had married, so it would appear that Marie had at least two children, Robert in 1947 and the baby that greeted Dad on his return home. Below Marie's address on the form was a space to list any children or stepchildren. It was left blank. We were never able to find any records of children being born to Dad and Marie and the blank space would suggest that they did not have any together. It had always puzzled me that they had no children, given she was a Catholic girl and they married in 1932. Even allowing for Dad's time away in the merchant navy and fighting the War, it was a surprise that there were no children. I had always supposed that, maybe, Marie was unable to bear children, but now there was evidence to suggest that she had two children. There were certainly no problems with Dad's ability to do his bit. Dad and Marie had got married when they were both still very young, Dad was still a teenager. Did they have to marry as Marie had got pregnant? If so, then there may possibly have been a problem with the pregnancy and the baby was never born. That might have discouraged them from trying to have any more children. I guessed I would never know but it did seem strange.

Reading that first page of the document, another thing struck me. It was dated January 1944. When Claire had told us the story of Dad's return from the war, I had assumed it would be much later than that: late 1944 or even 1945. The date was important as I had done some calculations on 'known' events, working backwards from the birth of my oldest brother, David, to try to figure out when Mum and Dad met. David was born in May 1948. Assuming Mum had a child, Carol, who was born at Christmas time but died very young, possibly at birth, that would mean that she was probably born in December 1946. Mum would be pregnant with David the following Christmas. Carol would have been conceived around March or April of 1946. Now, Claire told us that, after Dad discovered Marie's child, he had re-enlisted with the army and requested to be posted as far away as possible. She said he went to the Far East for two years. I was concerned that the arithmetic did not work out if Dad returned to Marie in 1945. That would mean he returned from the Far East in 1947 – too late to conceive Carol. Of course, it might be that Carol was not Dad's child anyway! However, Dad returning in January 1944 would lead to his return from his service in the Far East sometime in early 1946. Plenty of time for Dad to meet Mum and get her pregnant in time for Carol to be born at Christmas, later that year. I could not find any record of Carol being born on Ancestry UK so, either the birth and death was not registered (the baby may have died before birth) or the story of Carol was just another lie.

Michael, my youngest son, helped me to decipher some of the jargon on Arthur's records and, between us, we typed up a copy on a Word document so that it was easier to follow. This process helped us appreciate the timeline of his service and raised a few anomalies. We were not entirely sure that Dad returned home to Marie in January 1944, after all. It was then that he signed up as a commissioned officer in the army and was posted to the Middle East. This would contradict Claire's tale of his return to Marie, so it must have later in the War that he returned to the U.K. The record suggests that this was in May 1944 and that, in July of that year, he was granted an extension of the active list portion of his short service commission. He was posted to India in November 1944 and then to South-East Asia. He did not return to the U.K. until August 1946. That meant we were back to our original timeline of meeting Mum, so Carol was likely to be some else's child, not Dad's! Very confusing.

If Claire was correct about Dad going off to Burma after seeing Marie with her child, another of her stories about Dad's life in the army was not. The Allied invasion at Salerno, in Italy, took place in September 1943 but Dad was in the Middle East at that time. I had suspected something was amiss when I could not find his regiment listed in the book about the Salerno operation that I had purchased a few weeks earlier. It appeared that Dad joined the 78th (which became the 178) Medium Regiment in April 1944. Michael did some research on the 178 Medium Regiment and found that it was stuck behind the Gustav Line at Monte Cassino in Italy at that time. When I was young, I heard stories that Dad was part of the campaign to push the German army back from Cassino. The Allied forces had got bogged down in the Italian campaign at both Cassino and near the beach landings at Anzio. Claire had told us that Dad had spent a miserable Winter in trenches and that his commanding officer was George Sheen. Michael found that there was a George Turcan Chiene in the 178 Medium Regiment. He was surely the man that Claire was referring too, the name was too similar for it to be a coincidence. George had a very distinguished military career and was awarded the Distinguished Service Order. Part of his citation read: "Major George Chiene first distinguished himself in February 1944 in the Anzio bridgehead when his field battery was in direct support of the Loyals. Thanks to his resourcefulness and energy in breaking up enemy attacks by artillery fire, the battalion was saved from being overrun on several occasions. The battalion commander who was with him at battalion HQ, stated that his efficiency, coolness and cheerfulness in a tight corner were an inspiration to all around him and he gave the battalion "magnificent support" for a continuous period of two nights and one day"

This part of George's citation took place before Dad became his second-in-command, if he joined the regiment in April 1944, but it continues: "Later, in September 1944, when his battery was supporting 153 Infantry, US Army, the C.O. of that unit specially commended him for his excellent support and co-operative spirit. This commendation was endorsed by Lt. Gen. Mark Clark, Commander Fifth Army. These are two instances of the distinction with which Major Chiene has commanded his battery during the past year." Claire's telling of Arthur's experience in Italy suggested that Arthur and George were very close colleagues so I would like to think that Dad played a major part in helping George command his battery which such distinction. Dad did not get a Distinguished Service Order, but his records showed that he was awarded five medals: 1939-45 Star, Africa Star,

Italy Star, 1939-45 War Medal and Defence Medal, which were awarded in 1948 and 1949. I remember seeing some of Dad's medals when I was a child. I don't know what happened to them. They were either lost or, maybe, sold by Mum to raise some money, though I am not sure that they would have been worth much.

The final years of Dad's military career also made interesting reading when I linked the dates to what the family were doing. He was posted to Cyprus in March 1961 which, I believe, would be close to the time that the family moved to Sittingbourne in Kent, having lived briefly in Hastings after returning from Germany. He was in Cyprus for just over two years before relinquishing command on the completion of his service in May 1963, when he was granted the honorary rank of Lieutenant Colonel. I know that the family were told he was only going to Cyprus for six months, which is why we stayed in England and that Dad met Claire whilst on duty in Cyprus. I also found out, on my visit to Cryalls House, forty years after we left it, that it was regularly rented out to families of military personnel. With Dad no longer in the Army, I guess that we were told we would have to move out of the property. It was September 1963, four months later, that we moved to Eastnor in Herefordshire. I still do not know the reason that we moved to a completely new part of the country. My Dad had grown up in the London and the Home Counties and so did Mum, as far as I knew. So, what was the connection with Eastnor? The Gables, the house we went to live in there, belonged to the Eastnor Estate which, as far as I can remember, was owned by the Hervey-Bathurst family.

Major Hervey-Bathursts had a distinguished service in the Army so it might be that Dad found the house through his military connections. Another alternative, of course, is that there was some connection to Mum's family! Whatever the reason, it seemed that Dad wanted the family as far away as possible from him and, after the move to Herefordshire, there was very little contact between Mum and Dad. Dad was, by now, with Claire and, after leaving the army, began his life as a civilian in the catering business in Nottingham.

The only real chance of finding out who Mum was, would now be through the detective work of Tim as he tried to build up a family tree based on the Ancestry UK DNA results. I received a message from him that read; "Have made some progress with the Perry tree. Quite good evidence your mum may have been descended from either George Perry and Jane Barwell or Henry Perry and Mary Ann Barwell. If I could work out how they are related to Angharad Davies, who belongs to the Barwell side, I think we would be close enough to solve it". This was hugely encouraging and I went on Ancestry to study Tim's latest version of the Perry family tree. Much of the family appeared to be living in Australia. I suppose there is a chance that Mum was also from that part of the world, which is how she ended up by Lake Taupo in New Zealand, one of the stories she once told me. Tim had clearly already done plenty of research on the families of both couples he had mentioned in his message, but I still did some of my own work on Ancestry. I came across a picture of one Maria Perry. I could see many features of Mum in her appearance or was I just looking too hard to find them in the hope that that we were close to cracking the mystery? It might be wishful thinking, but I felt that it would not be too long before I got a message from Tim to say that he'd found Mum.

We decided that it would make a lovely present for Claire in Malta if we were to collect some family photos together and put them in a book. We had already used an online company before to do this, so it was just a matter of sorting some photos and adding some text. My aim was to include as many members of the family as possible so she could see what they looked like. I wanted to start the book with the old black and white photos we had, then have a page or two for Dad, Mum and each of the six children with their children. The process of selecting pictures made me realise how few pictures we had of the family, particularly from the early days. There was not a single photo of all six children, mainly due to David's self-imposed exile from the rest of us for forty years. There is a picture from around 1958, with the five eldest children, before Colin was born. When we visited David in the 1990s, Bob did not come with us, so there are pictures of four of us, including David, together (the fifth person took the picture- the days before selfies!). I tried to rectify the lack of a full group picture by putting a picture of the five of us, taken at Mum's funeral, on the front cover of the book and included a picture of David in an inserted frame below us. I also did the same to add Mum and Dad to the front page. The entire family united, at last! Of course, we had lost many of our photos in the past, particularly when the biscuit tin, that held some, was lost by Bob when he moved in Hereford. I do not, however, remember ever seeing any pictures that had Mum and Dad together. Indeed, I don't recall many, if any, of Mum when she was quite young. The earliest photo of Mum is when she was at Peta's wedding in 1968. In the picture book, Mum's page was facing the page for Dad. I decided to choose photos which meant that they were facing each other across the page divide. When I had finished composing the pictures, I looked at Mum looking across to the image of Dad and wondered what they might be saying to each other if they met now? Mum only spent about 15 years of her long life with Dad but had six, possibly seven children with him in that short time. What was their relationship like and what led to the eventual separation?

It wasn't only the relationship between Mum and Dad that I thought about. It seemed that Dad had had quite a troubled time with most of the women in his life. He had, after all, ran away from home, apparently, at the age of six because he wanted to get away from his 'evil stepmother'. I know, from his marriage certificate to Marie, that his father, Leonard Brasier Lovering, was present at the ceremony, but what about his mother Catherine (Kate) Grindlay? I went back to the Ancestry website to remind myself of the dates and details of Leonard's life. I then realised that he did not marry Ethel, the evil stepmother, until March 1923, the same month that Kate died. That would suggest that he was 'living in sin' with Ethel, prior to then. They had a child, Violet, in 1919. Dad was born in 1913 so he would have been six in 1919, the age when he supposedly ran away. Did Leonard move out of his home with Kate, to live with Ethel, and took Arthur with him and, possibly Sidney, Arthur's older brother, too? If Sidney went as well, then I wondered what he thought of his Dad's new woman and what was his reaction when Arthur then ran away from home? I guess we'll never know but it was certainly a complicated situation. I used Ancestry to find out if there was any more information about Kate. The records included some of the Electoral registers. I was astonished to find that, according to the records, Kate was still living with Leonard right up to her death in 1923. The records for each year between 1919 and 1922 had Kate and Leonard in the same household, along with George Lovering and Elizabeth Lovering. I can only assume that George and Elizabeth were Leonard's older brother and his wife. What was going on? Did Kate move out and go to live with her brother-in-law and they recorded Leonard as living there too just to avoid a scandal?

I investigated the records of both Ethel and Violet further. There was some uncertainty about the entries on Ancestry. It is quite common that there are several people with similar names living at the same time. As far as I could ascertain, Violet was born on 15th November 1919. Her mother's maiden name, however, was given as Smith. Now this either means that I've got the wrong record or Ethel preferred to register her name as Smith, rather than Lewis. Of course, it might be that Violet's mother was not Ethel after all and that Leonard had got another woman pregnant instead! The 1939 census shows that Violet was still living with both of her parents. Leonard died in 1946 but it seems that Violet stayed with Ethel for several years afterwards. Both women eventually got married. Ethel became Ethel Price and eventually died in 1997 having reached the age of one hundred years old. Violet married a chap named Woodward in January 1973 in Brixworth, Northamptonshire.

Whatever was happening between Leonard, Kate and Ethel, it clearly had a huge impact on my Dad's life as it led to him going to Greenwich and becoming a merchant seaman. His Dad fathering a child out of wedlock must also have made an impression on Arthur as he was to encounter similar problems in his life. He and Marie were quite young when they got married so I believe there is a strong possibility that they had to get married. In other words, Arthur got Marie pregnant and decided that it was the right thing to make it legitimate and tie the knot. I suspect that there was a problem with the pregnancy which led to a termination. Perhaps Marie was then told that she would not be able to bear any children. If this is true, that would have been devastating for both of them. It appeared that Dad remained with Marie right up to that fateful day when he returned from fighting in Italy in 1944. For much of that time, however, Dad might well have been away from home, either sailing in the banana boat or engaging with the German forces. According to Claire, he was very upset when he found Marie with another man's child, but I do wonder whether they had drifted apart long before then.

After re-enlisting with the Army and being 'posted as far away as possible' for two years, Dad returned to England to work in the War Office. One night, I suggest, he was enjoying himself in a club or pub and got chatting to the woman working behind the bar. The relationship blossomed and the woman found herself pregnant. That woman being Mum (Helen?). Once again, Arthur found himself in an awkward position but, this time, he could not do the honorable thing, and get married. He was already married to Marie and had no desire to track her down. Did he tell Helen, 'I can't marry you because I am already married!'. The solution was for Helen to assume Marie's identity which led to the mystery of Mum's true background.

Twenty years later, Dad had met a new woman in Cyprus, Claire Foster. He got her pregnant, again out of wedlock. Once again, he would like to do the right thing but has to explain, again, 'I can't marry you because I am already married to Marie!'. That pregnancy also terminated early but, thanks to the letter out of the blue from Marie, he was able to marry Claire in 1965. They lived very happily together until Dad died in 1982. Perhaps he had found the love of his life at last. Just as Mum had found true love with Mike in her final years, I would like to think that both Mum and Dad ended their lives in a good place.

10 HELEN

I was watching a programme on BBC television called *'Family Finders'*. I was always interested in programmes about genealogy and would regularly chip in with comments relating to my own research into family details. This programme was looking to find what happened to a sister who had been adopted in the 1930s. The expert on the film stated that when a woman became pregnant out of wedlock in the 1930s and 1940s, there were basically three options. She could have the pregnancy terminated, though it was illegal at the time. She could marry the father or she could have the baby adopted (adoption had become legal in the 1920s due to the rising number of single mothers as a result of the First World War). I immediately added: "or she can just pretend to be the wife of the father and carry on as normal!".

I was still waiting to hear if Tim had worked out who Mum was using the DNA analysis. The family tree he had created was growing larger and he would occasionally notify me of the additions. It appeared most likely that Mum was from the Perry/Barwell family, many of whom had settled in or been born and raised in Australia. New matches also appeared on my Ancestry DNA link. I studied any new additions and eliminated those that were on Dad's side and then messaged some of the others. I would explain that I was trying to identify Mum and asked if there were any Helens, Hildas or Audreys in their family who were born in the 1920s and grew up in London. I got a few replies, including one from Australia, but, sadly, they were not able to help.

Another television programme that caught my attention was called '*Mrs Wilson*'. It was a drama about the true story of a woman who married a man who worked for the Secret Service during the second world war. She was happily married for many years but, unfortunately, one day her husband had a heart attack and dropped down dead. The woman was then surprised to find that, at the funeral, another woman turned up who claimed to be his wife as well. It turned out that he had actually married (at least) three women, each one completely ignorant of the existence of other wives! My interest was not only in the fact that the man was a bigamist, something I had thought that Dad was at one time, but that it illustrated the secrets and intrigue that were prevalent during that period of history. In the case of my family, Michael, my son, had one theory that maybe Mum was a spy! She had claimed to have been in Germany, at the Nuremburg rallies, and also to have lived in the Soviet Union and could speak Russian. Possibly the reason that we were unable to trace her real identity was that she was not a British national at all and had used several aliases during her life. She had got pregnant with Dad so she might have access to vital data and information within the Ministry of Defence which could be useful to the Kremlin. It was vital that her cover was not blown and that was why some documents about her had disappeared. Michael reckoned that it was no coincidence that the family photographs had gone missing from Bob's house and then, years later, Claire lost her photographs in Malta.

It seemed a very fanciful idea to imagine that Mum was a Russian spy but the story about *'Mrs Wilson'* did make me re-assess the idea of bigamy. As stated previously, we had thought that Dad might have been a bigamist but, then discovered that he divorced Marie Cremin before marrying Claire Foster. What had not occurred to me was that Mum might be a bigamist, or, at least, been charged with bigamy. Mum had assumed the identity of Marie Cremin, who was married to Dad. The real Marie Cremin got a divorce from Dad and re-married in 1969. That meant, that according to official records, Marie Lovering was no more, she had become Mrs Marie Murray. Meanwhile, in Ledbury in 1970, Mrs Marie Lovering – the false one, my Mum – was getting married to Mike Barnes. Anyone checking their family history about the Lovering family would be surprised to find that Marie Lovering had got married to two different men in successive years and would not be able to locate any record of another Marie Lovering existing. Thus, they would conclude that Marie Lovering was a bigamist. I wonder if Mum was aware that Dad had managed to divorce the original Marie or that she had re-married in Bournemouth. I doubt it and it probably did not worry Mum that she might, technically, had committed the crime of bigamy. Most of her life had been a huge lie and she had created a long line of falsehoods whilst recognising that the real Marie could turn up at any time. The other question that arises, just as '*Mrs Wilson*' discovered, is that were there any more Marie Loverings out there?

Out of curiosity, I decided to order a copy of the death certificate of my grandfather, Leonard Brasier Lovering. I had done frequent searches on the internet to see if I could find out where he was buried. I had found nothing. Perhaps he had been cremated. I wondered whether his death certificate might reveal anything new to me. It would certainly tell me the cause of his death, something I had not thought about before. I assumed that he had died a natural death due to old age. The certificate duly arrived a week later and confirmed that my grandad had died on 22nd October 1946 at St Luke's Hospital in London and that he was a retired printer. The cause of death was given as 'carcinoma of the lung, carcinoma of stomach and omentum'. So, he had died of cancer of the lungs and stomach, not just old age. The informant of the death was given as 'A. W. Lovering, Capt., Son, 8 Devonshire Terrace W2'. It was my father. I was aware from electoral registers that Dad was registered as being at 95 Portland Road which was where my grandad lived. He obviously registered his name there as a matter of convenience as he was clearly not staying in the same place for long. I had not come across the Devonshire Terrace address before. I looked it up on a map and found that it is very close to Paddington Station and that I had passed it many times. It might have been around the time of my grandad's death that Dad had met my Mum, Helen. Maybe Helen also lived at that address in Devonshire Terrace too. I eagerly checked the electoral registers for the post-war years to see if there were any women registered who could conceivably be Mum. Not for the first time, I ended up being disappointed. Rather surprisingly, there were twenty people listed at the property. I assume that the building was split into apartments. Among those listed were Mabel, Rona, Daphne, Ethel, Nora, Lillian, Catherine, Shelagh, Margaret, Iris, Lillian and Jean. Some of the women shared surnames with others so were clearly part of a family unit there. Was Dad living with any of the others and was Mum one of them? None of the names would suggest that Mum was amongst them but, perhaps, even the Helen and Hilda Audrey names were fictional. Dad had only been back in England for two months, following his service in South-East Asia, when his father died. In his will, Leonard Brasier Lovering left all his effects of £217 14s. 6d. to his son, Arthur. It is not clear whether Leonard owned the house that he lived in, but Arthur remained registered on the electoral register until 1948, by which time, of course, he would have met Mum.

I had, by now, visited Malta three times in less than a year, and another visit was on the horizon. I had found out much about my Dad from Claire, both from the Malta trips and her letters. We had continued to exchange letters about once a fortnight for over a year. In her more recent letters, Claire had begun to tell me more about her own family. Her father, Major William Foster, M.C., T.D., J.P., had fought in France during the first world war and was awarded the Military Cross for bravery. Simon would have been proud of him! Claire told me that, like many others who fought in that war, he did not like to talk about his experiences. In 1918, his regiment, the Sherwood Foresters, was posted in Ireland to put down the rebellion there, that would, eventually, lead to an independent Ireland. His regiment was marching through Dublin led by a boy soldier and a ram, the regiment's mascot. Suddenly, both the boy and the animal were shot dead by bullets coming from the second-floor window of a building nearby. Claire's father was beside himself with rage and dashed up the stairs to confront the perpetrators. He rushed into the room, followed by some of his men. The rebels were still looking out of the window and were laughing at the confusion below. A fight ensued and the rebels soon gave in and were captured. William's Commanding Officer wanted to put his name forward for a medal to reward his bravery but, as Ireland was still part of the United Kingdom, no military medals were able to be awarded. During the second world war, William was in a searchlight position and later transferred to London, where he was employed as a translator as he spoke fluent French. Claire's mother was an air raid warden during the second world war, whilst Claire helped with the medical services. Her younger sister, Shirley, was still at school.

Claire's parents worked hard for their community, and both were recognised in the Queen's Honours lists. Claire informed me that her father was awarded the O.B.E and her mother the C.B.E. Even her sister was given an honour, the M.B.E. I tried find the citations for these honours on the internet but was only able to find information about her mother's C.B.E, which she was awarded in 1964, 'for political and public services in Nottingham'.

In another letter, Claire described the trauma of her grandmother's early life. Elise Gsell was born in Alsace in France, which bordered the new state of Germany. Claire remembered that, when she was small, she was told to hate the Germans! Claire wrote,

"The reason was because, in 1870, the Germans invaded Alsace and her grandmother's family had to flee to Paris. Granny's first memory, as a child of five years old, was the horror of the journey after being forced to leave her happy home. Apparently, the train was packed and everyone was fighting for a seat. She was very frightened, especially as the train was regularly bumping about. Granny's intense dislike of the Germans was reinforced during the second world war when, once again, Germany invaded Alsace. By then, however, granny was staying with a friend in London where she died before France was liberated."

Claire's granny had also been a servant of the community, having been the Lady Mayoress of Nottingham. Claire's grandfather, Edward L. Manning was the Lord Mayor of Nottingham in 1922/23. All these stories encouraged me to do some further research into Claire's family on Ancestry and I was able to send her details of several generations on her mother's side. Her father's side of the family was more difficult as there were several men called William Foster in the Nottingham area at that time. I would require more information to track down his ancestors. It would also be interesting to find out more about her father's military service, particularly in the first world war but, once again, I needed more details about him, his date of birth, etc.

When I visited Malta next, I had a few days there on my own before Pauline and Michael joined me. On the way to watch some Maltese football matches in Paola, not far from Valletta, I broke my journey on the bus so I could visit the Addolorata Cemetery. Claire had told me previously that her sister was buried in this cemetery and I wanted to find her grave. Apparently, when Shirley died, Claire was initially told that no more burials were permitted in the cemetery. However, since there was already a plot where her parents were laid to rest, then Shirley could join them. It had been a while since I had been grave searching in a cemetery and I realised that it might be a fruitless task. As I approached the gates, I could see how big the cemetery was so it would be impossible to locate the grave on my own unless I was very fortunate. My luck was in as the cemetery office was open. Not only was the kind gentleman in the office able to tell me where to find the grave, he also gave me a copy of a map of the cemetery. There were two burial ceremonies in progress as I walked to the far side of the cemetery to the Foster grave. The paths were very uneven and the cemetery was on a hillside. It must have been very difficult for Claire when she attended Shirley's funeral. It did not help that there were also some stone steps to descend to reach the grave plot. Thanks to the map, it was relatively easy to locate the plot and I was able to read the names inscribed on the stone slab over the grave: 'WILLIAM FOSTER 1896-1981' and 'AGNETA LINA

FOSTER 1901-1988'. I now had William's year of birth which would help for my research into his past. I studied the grave carefully and looked all around. There was no inscription to indicate that Shirley was also buried there. When I met Claire, two days later, she asked if I had got to the cemetery and she was quite pleased when I was able to show her some pictures that I had taken. It was, obviously, impossible for her to visit the grave herself though she said that her very old friend, Guido, did visit occasionally. I said it would be good to get Shirley's name added to the inscription, if possible. It just did not seem right that someone who had led such a rich life should be buried, effectively, in an unmarked grave.

My visit to Malta did not yield any further information about my Dad but there was a lovely surprise when we visited Claire at her home at Villa Messina in Rabat. I had not noticed it before but, on the wall above Claire's bed, was a simple painting of some flowers. It was signed 'A.W.L.' It had been painted by my father who had his own 'man shed' at their home where he would spend hours with his artwork. I did not know that he was keen on art but both Bob and Colin had excelled in that skill, as well. Despite Pauline's reservations about my claim to be good at art too, I frequently reminded her that I came top in the Art exam in my first year at Ledbury Grammar School, with my 'Pylons to the British Camp' masterpiece. I got 70% for that work. In the second-year exam, I got 50% and then 40% in the third year. I quit Art after, I could see where it was going! It was still a thrill to see something produced by my father's own hands.

Seeing the painting by Dad made me realise that there were still things around to remind us of the past and people who are no longer with us. Unfortunately, many treasured photos had been lost, both at Bob's and by Claire in Malta. It made me remember, however, that I still had some video film of family events of the past. In particular, I had borrowed the school video camera so that I was able to film the wedding of Simon and Karen in 1991. I dug out the video and, having purchased the necessary equipment, I was able to convert the video into a digital format which made viewing simpler. It was quite moving to watch the video. The loss of Simon was still quite hard to accept and there he was, in the video, on the biggest day of his life, getting married to Karen. All the family attended so there was also film of Bob with his cheeky asides to the camera. Mum featured prominently and it was moving to see Mum again and to hear her voice. There is one moment when she is getting quite frustrated when trying to take a photo and gives that Mum look at the video camera. It was precious to have that film of Simon, Bob and Mum at such a happy occasion and they appeared just how we remembered them. We all looked so young, but our characters shone through. The film was rather long, mainly due to Colin's Best Man speech which did go on a bit! I decided to edit the video down to about four or five minutes and then posted it on YouTube so that anyone in the family, or in the world, could view it. It then occurred to me that Claire would enjoy watching it as well. She would be delighted to see Bob, as she knew him quite well, but it would also provide an opportunity for her to 'meet' the rest of the family. The only problem was that I did not have access to the internet at Claire's home at Villa Messina in Malta. Andre, who dealt with Claire's affairs, had informed me that not even the staff were told the password for the wifi system in the home! The next time I visited Claire, I asked at the reception for the wifi password. Andre was correct, the receptionist was not able to give it to me but suggested that I went to see the manager in his office. I found the door to his office, tapped gently on the door and opened it. He was sat at his desk and I explained who I was and that I would like the password, if that was possible. He immediately rose and walked towards me to greet me. "It is so nice to meet you, at last!", he exclaimed, "I was really intrigued when I received the email from you, via the church, explaining that you were trying to trace your father's widow. I am really pleased that Claire has discovered her family!". Armed with the password, I was able to share the video with Claire who was, at last, able to see some of her newly discovered family.

A few months later, I was reminded that there would be another movie legacy of my late brother, Simon. Shortly before he died, he had become an actor! He was a friend of a guy who was making a film, called '*Weapon*', about the psychological repercussions of soldiers returning from warzones. Simon had been given a part in the film where he played the part of a psychoanalyst which involved quite a lot of dialogue. Simon was relieved that he did not have to memorise all his words as he was able to hold a clipboard as part of his role. His words were on the clipboard. The film had taken a long time to complete and I was beginning to think it would never see the light of day. Then, one day, a trailer appeared for the film. There, in a millisecond glimpse, was Simon! It was several months before the film was finally released on Amazon Prime (it did not get a cinema release). Simon was involved in several scenes and I was quite proud of his performance. There was a dedication to him in the credits.

Treasuring memories of lost ones became even more pertinent a few weeks later. My brother, David, had been having a few issues with his health. He had long needed a walking stick to help himself around Ashford in Kent, but he was now becoming increasingly breathless and his legs had swollen. He needed to have lots of medical tests. Fortunately, he was able to get to his doctors quite easily but some of the tests involved a trip to the hospital in Canterbury. One afternoon, David rang me. He sounded quite down. He told me that his doctor had phoned him at home one evening with some bad news. David was informed that he had cancer of the blood and that the doctors would not be able to treat it. Then the bombshell landed, as David was told that he would probably only live for another six months to a year! I was truly shocked by the news. Okay, David was seventy-one years old, he had survived ten years longer than both Bob and Simon, but it was devastating news and I found it very hard to know what to say. David, quite naturally, appeared to be in a state of shock too but some of the Lovering humour and resilience shone through. He had previously had a health scare during the London Olympics in 2012 and, being a sports fanatic, he declared that he was determined to live long enough to see the Tokyo Olympics in 2020, some ten months later. I admired his spirit. He also pointed out that Peta had told us she had been given six months to live and that was over fifteen years before. She was still alive and kicking! I felt a little helpless living so far away from him in Bristol but was reassured that his friends nearby were looking after him. I had already arranged to visit him a couple of weeks later so I would then be able to see the state of his health for myself. Colin's sixtieth birthday was approaching, and he was returning to the UK to celebrate it. I was really pleased when he said that he wanted to visit David as well. Simon never wanted anything to do with David and Colin had always put off making contact. It would be wonderful to get my oldest and youngest brothers together again for the first time in over fifty years.

Before Colin's birthday, I also celebrated a significant landmark in my life. I reached my sixty-second birthday. Apart from being a year older, that birthday would not have meant much to me, except that neither Bob nor Simon reached that age, both passing away whilst they were sixty-one. Indeed, I had spent the entire year since my sixty-first birthday telling everyone that my target was to reach my next birthday. Although I am sure that people tired of my negative outlook, I should add that I bought a Senior Railcard for a three-year period (it saved money) which proved I was optimistic of lasting beyond the age of sixty-one and I also bought a diary for 2020. Nevertheless, it was a relief to finally make it to the grand old age of sixty-two. Reaching that landmark also made me reflect on the fact that it was now about thirty -seven years since we had started down the road to find out who Mum was, and that little progress was being made. I had been writing this account of the mystery for well over a year and wondering whether I would ever get an ending. It did not look promising. I had printed off everything completed so far and given copies to both Claire, in Malta, and Pauline to read. I had done some proof reading prior to that which reminded me of some the stories in the family. I had told how Dad had married Marie at a young age and suggested that they possibly had to get married as Marie was pregnant but, as we found no record of a birth, that the pregnancy had gone wrong. There was also the story that Mum gave birth to a child, Carol, who died at a young age and that Mum was told that she would not be able to have any more children. She ended up with six.

Re-reading these tales led me to a strange thought. Maybe, it was Marie who was told that she would not be able to have any children and that would make Dad doubly annoyed to return home from fighting in Italy to find his wife with a child. Not only had she been unfaithful but had achieved something with her lover that he was not able to do! Maybe, when he got Mum pregnant and she assumed Marie's identity, Mum used some parts of Marie's life as part of the fabrication. Was it Marie or Mum who was told she could no longer bear children? We shall probably never find out, but both women proved the doctors wrong. How much of Marie's life story did Mum take on board? Mulling over that thought jogged my memory. I recalled another thing Mum had told us when we were young. We had always joked about her being Irish and I had asked her why she was born in Ireland when she had told us that she grew up in London. She had replied that her parents were on holiday in Cork at the time. I am sure that that many people have given birth whilst on holiday, but it seemed an unlikely thing, even to us, despite being quite young at the time. It was clear that, even before Mum admitted that she and Dad were not married, that we had our suspicions about her story.

The day before I was due to meet Colin in London to visit David, I received a rather strange email from a friend of David's. It was from someone who called himself Honkey Roy. I had, in fact, received a message from him, via Ancestry, a few days previously. Several months earlier, I had come across a family tree, on Ancestry, which was named after my father. I was, naturally, very curious and had sent a message to the owner of the tree. Honkey Roy replied to apologise for not answering sooner and explained that it was him that had done the family research on behalf of David. I had seen the results of his detective work when I had visited David and it made interesting reading but did not include anything I did not know already. Roy was a good friend of David's and, now that David had been diagnosed with a terminal condition, I had given Roy my email address so that he could keep me informed of David's progress. The email read:

"David is due to visit the local Hospice (Pilgrims Hospice, Willesborough, Ashford) on Dec 05 between 10:30 – 12:30hr. They would like a 'Lasting Power of Attorney'. I suggested you, sorry to drop you in it! David has recently put Peta's name down as Next of Kin at his Doctor's Surgery. The Hospice is just a ten-minute bus ride from Ashford Town Centre, though David said that his friend Ian has agreed to take him there – I just hope that David does not sign Lasting Power of Attorney over to Ian."

Roy went on to express his feelings about Ian and told me his background. Ian had been due to go on trial for having under-age sex with girls and had gone on the run to Africa to escape the law. He contracted malaria and, when the authorities in Sierra Leone discovered he was an illegal immigrant, he was deported back to Britain. He was convicted of his offences and sent to prison.

Well, I was rather taken aback to hear what Roy had to say. I had met Ian and he seemed a very pleasant person. I was not sure how much I could rely on Roy's information and, anyway, it was for David to decide about who should be his power of attorney. I thanked Roy for letting me know and that I would try to raise the issue of power of attorney with David when we visited him the next day.

I met Colin at St Pancras International station and we discussed the email whilst on the train journey to Ashford International. I told Colin not to mention any of it to David, particularly as Roy did not want David to know that he had been in contact with me. If the facts in the email were correct, it did, of course, raise the question of whether David was aware of Ian's activities at the time. We were so engrossed in the discussion that I had not noticed that we had got on the wrong train and would not arrive in Ashford for another two hours! We got off the train at Strood, caught a train back to Ebbsfleet and then another to Ashford. I was pleased to see Colin and David meeting again after such a long time although the circumstances could have been better. David showed us the letter from his doctor which outlined his ailments and which clearly stated that treatment for them would not be beneficial. It gave David six to twelve months to live. The letter also suggested that David was put in the hands of the hospice to help him prepare for 'end of life'. I asked David to give my contact details to the hospice although I did not explicitly mention power of attorney. David explained that the woman who lived in the flat below was aware of his condition and that he could bang on the floor if he needed help. She had a key to his flat so would be able to come up to see if he had a problem. Apparently, the builders, working in the flat above David, one day, dropped something on the floor. A moment later, the woman from below was ringing David to check that he was all right! We spent over an hour with David before we felt it was best to leave David in peace. He suffered greatly from breathlessness so found it very demanding to talk at length. Walking back to the station, Colin thanked me for going with him to see David. He was really pleased that the three of us had been reunited, at last.

The next day, I received another email from Roy:

"David phoned me yesterday afternoon, emotionally breaking down, I couldn't make any sense what-so-ever of what he was saying on the phone so I went round to see if he was alright last evening, by which time he had got himself together a bit. I guess it all got a bit much but he did say that the visit (or 'The Royal Visit' as he calls it, which is Lovering humour me thinks) went as well as can be expected.

I asked if he talked about the 'Lasting Power of Attorney' issue: First I got a sharp 'No!' – And then he said, Well yes, he is going to name your good self, Peta & Ian."

Roy then gave me further details about Ian. When Ian was released from prison, only David and Ian's mother wanted anything to do with him. David cooked meals for Ian, who in turn bought some furniture for David. Roy went on to say,

"David did show me your draft family history book: much impressed- you have put in a good many hours. Love the humour. And yes, I thought exactly the same, when David showed me the photo that you kindly sent him of 'Mum' (David having previously said to me, 'Was my mother my mother?) – I said, 'God, you look so much like your Mother – David, This is definitely your Mother!'

P.S. Ian has a key to David's apartment, as does Ansley (the lady in the basement apartment directly beneath David, as do the builders currently working in the top floor apartment directly above David and also Frank Gen the Landlord – but he resides mainly in London."

It was another interesting email, but rather disturbing to hear more about Ian's past. Whatever Ian's personality and background, he did appear to have David's best interests in mind and had done much to help him in his hour of need. In some ways I felt a little reassured to know that there were several people keeping an eye on David.

I met up with Colin again, a few days after our visit to

David, to join other members of the family to celebrate Colin's birthday at the Feathers Hotel in Ledbury. The same hotel that we had stayed in on our first visit to Herefordshire in 1963 and where David had worked for a while after leaving college. A few of Colin's old friends from his days of living in Ledbury also came to congratulate him. One of them was a man I used to teach when I started my career at John Masefield High School. He assured me that he was good at maths so it would appear I did him no harm with my inexperienced teaching! I got talking to Peta about David and his illness. I told her that he was very down about it but had joked that he might survive longer than a year as she had done. Peta looked confused. I reminded her about when she was ill. Peta said that she did not remember that! Now I was confused. Peta had told us that she had been given only six months to live and now she could not recall being given such a diagnosis. I had got annoyed when Mum had followed Mike to Scotland within weeks of him turning up again out of the blue after many years away. I had wondered how Mum could abandon her daughter in her hour of need. I now realised that maybe Mum knew that Peta was not terminally ill after all. Later, I spoke to James and his wife, Emma, about his Mum's 'illness' and he confirmed that she was not telling us the entire truth about her situation all those years before. I suspected that Peta had made more of her ailment than was merited or that there had been a complete misunderstanding over what Peta had told us.. James also mentioned going to the funeral of Mike, Mum's husband, in Scotland. I did not attend Mike's funeral and was surprised that James had made the long journey.

I had messaged Tim (again!) about progress on the DNA research and he said we needed more '3rd cousin' matches if we were to make more progress. I ordered a DNA kit for Peta in the hope that we might get some new matches. I was visiting Hereford a few days after Colin's celebrations to watch York City play. I called in to see Peta in Ledbury and got her to give a DNA sample to send off. We got talking about Mike's funeral again and I said I was surprised that James had gone since he hardly knew Mike. Peta revealed that she and Steve had visited Mum and Mike in Scotland on several occasions. I had not imagined Steve making the long journey up to Kirriemuir as he had rarely travelled anywhere in his life. I don't ever recall being aware that Peta and members of her family had travelled up North so that was yet another 'secret' to me! It appears that they used all sorts of transport, going up by plane on one occasion. Peta also informed me that Jan, Bob's widow, no longer wanted to meet up with her. I told Peta that it was probably due to the Malta connection and that she felt a little embarrassed about her and Bob travelling out to see Claire and Shirley without telling the rest of the family. Peta thought there must be more to it than just that, so I told her about Tim's education being partly paid for by Claire and Shirley.

Peta had to leave to fetch Izzy from school which gave me an opportunity to have a chat with Steve. We somehow got to talking about his family and he told me that his sister Sybil did not approve when he had married Peta in 1968. Sybil thought that Peta was not good enough for Steve. I think the fact that Peta was pregnant at the time of the wedding might have had something to do with her opinion. Steve then went on to say that he had not had contact with his sister for several years and only found out by chance that her husband had died. I was slightly taken aback by this as I remembered seeing quite a lot of Sybil when I had lived in Colwall with Peta and Steve in the 1970s. I told Steve that he should try to repair the relationship with his sister and compared it to what had happened with David and us. Steve's Mum was a Jehovah's Witness and had died several years before. Steve continued talking about his wedding and explained that his Mum had agreed to pay for the reception as my Mum was unable to afford it. It was usual for the bride's parents to bear the major burden of the cost of a wedding in those days and, since Dad would have nothing to do with his daughter's wedding, it was impossible for Mum to pay. What Steve told me next was yet another huge surprise. He revealed that his Mum had hired a private detective to investigate whether my Mum was telling the truth about her financial situation. Wow! I would love to know what the private detective discovered and thought that maybe the report might still exist somewhere. If it did, then Sybil probably had possession of it. That was another good reason for Steve to make up with his sister.

A couple of days before I visited Peta, we had heard that David had been admitted to hospital. Apparently, he had been unable to stand up so had contacted his doctor. Peta had been in touch with the hospital who told her that David was a little confused and disorientated and that they would be keeping him a little longer. The next day, I received a phone call from David. It was very difficult to understand what he was saying. He sounded very depressed and confused, but it was good to hear from him, nevertheless. I did not know it, but it would the last time that I would speak to him. The hospital told us that David had picked up a urinary infection and had an infection of lungs which meant his stay in hospital would be extended. On Sunday, 8th December 2019, I got a phone call from Peta. David had passed away. The news came as a shock as I had not expected him to go so quickly. Indeed, I had been discussing his illness with Colin and said that it could be a long, drawn-out demise. I was relieved that he did not have to suffer for months. The family tree had lost another leaf. I was now the eldest brother left.

Peta had heard the news of David's death, not from the hospital, but from his friend, Ian. Ian had told the hospital that he was David's nephew, so they gave all David's personal belongings to him. The story confirmed what David's other close friend had told me: that Ian was a rather devious person. On the other hand, supposing Ian really was David's nephew. That would open another intriguing chapter to the Lovering story. Was he a secret child of Bob or Simon or possibly of one of Marie's children? I concluded that it was just Ian telling lies.

After the initial shock of the news, I realised that, although Peta had been named as next of kin, it would be me that would have to sort out David's funeral and other affairs. The next day, I received an email from David's friend, Roy, the gardener. It read:

"Hi again Rick, really sorry to bring this up at this time but Ansley has just text me to say that Ian is in David's apartment, banging about right at this moment!".

I didn't know what was going on, but it was not something I expected on the day after David's death. The next day, Roy sent another message:

"Good morning Rick, I have just spoken to Frank Gen, David's Landlord, who is in Tenerife at the moment. I have informed him of David's passing and that Ian changed the locks on the interior door to David's apartment last Monday evening. Frank Gen is not happy - saying that what Ian has done is illegal - changing the locks without the landlord's knowledge or permission."

In a later email, I found out that Ian may have taken a table from David's flat as well as some bags of stuff. Ansley, the woman who lived in the flat below David's, had called the police to report the break-in and they had stopped him returning. The table was, according to Roy, one of the most valuable items in the flat. I did not really want to have to deal with the police. I just wanted to sort David's things which, of course, involved having to look through his flat for various documents regarding pension, bank, utilities, etc. I booked the train tickets to Ashford, as well as an overnight stay at a B&B. Since it was possible that Ian had changed the lock on David's flat, I contacted him and arranged to meet at the flat at 1pm. I rang David's landlord who had instructed his builders, working in the flat above, to replace the lock to the outside door so Ian could not get in. He would tell the builders to let me in, however, when I met Ian. Whilst on the train to Ashford, Roy sent more information to help pass the journey. It told me more about David's life and his relationship with Ian. It read,

"David worked for many a year for a business man with a small chain of music record shops: Parrot Records, Southend (David lived in Southend for quite a few years), Basildon (commuted to work in Basildon shop from Southend), Chelmsford, Colchester (David lived in Colchester for three years). And, of course, then Canterbury where he met Ian and his girlfriend."

He went on to describe what happened after David moved to Canterbury. "For whatever reason, David began taking money from the till at the record shop. The owner got suspicious (but at first could not believe that it was David after many a year as a loyal employee) but the evidence was overwhelming after a while. David was prosecuted but, as a first offence and previously of good character, was let off with a community sentence, working in a charity shop. David could only have been about fifty years old, but he never got another job! No references and no work history to show an employer – went to live with Ian in Margate/Ramsgate for a couple of years, a short while in Folkestone, and then moved into Ashford – I think 2002. David got by on dole money until he was sixty: by that time there had been the European Court Ruling / Case which said that a man had to be paid the same as a woman of the same age – so David got Pension Credit – He was overjoyed!"

It appeared that David had been encouraged to dip his fingers into the till and that had led to the end of his career working in record shops. It was disappointing to hear. David had got into trouble over money and, like Bob when he worked in a department store in Hereford, had abused his position to steal from his employers. Money issues caused a lot of problems for the Lovering family!

I arrived at David's flat a little early, so I called on Ansley who lived in a flat below David. She explained what had happened when Ian broke into David's flat. She had only met Ian once before and felt very uncomfortable in his presence. I left my bag with her as Ansley invited me back for a cup of tea after I had sorted the flat. When I went up the steps to David's flat, Ian was waiting for me. The builders let us into the house and Ian handed me a brand-new key so I could enter through the door to David's flat. Ian denied that he had changed the locks but there was clearly some damage around the lock, as well as a small toolkit just inside, on the floor. I immediately noticed that the table in the middle of David's front room had gone. It was also noticeable that the shelves with DVDs in front of the fireplace had been moved. Something that was hidden there had obviously been removed. Was it cash, some incriminating evidence or something else? To be honest, I really did not wish to know. Ian pointed to where David's documents were kept and told me David's naughty magazines were in the bottom drawer. As I searched through the documents, Ian and I talked about David. Ian was close to tears at times. He clearly had deep feelings for David despite his wrongdoings of the past. I found bank statements, gas bills and other things that I would need to sort out David's finances, as well as his old passport. It was a little worrying to see that David appeared to permanently over-drawn at his bank by five to eight hundred pounds. Amongst the documents, I also came across copies of some old newspapers which reported on Ian being found guilty of his crimes, following his extradition from Sierra Leone when he contracted malaria. I made sure that Ian did not see them.

After an hour, Ian had to leave, which was a relief, as I was then able to concentrate on searching the rest of the flat. I enjoyed my cup of tea with Ansley and then checked into my accommodation in the centre of Ashford. That evening, I phoned Co-op Funeralcare to arrange David's cremation. I had opted for a cremation without ceremony which would mean there would be no formal funeral service. Ironically, the cremation would take place in Sittingbourne, a couple of miles from where the family had lived in the early 1960s. The following day, I returned to the flat to tidy a few more things then travelled by bus to the hospital where David had died. Unfortunately, the doctors' certificates were not ready. It meant that I would have to travel back to Ashford, two days later, to collect them, before catching a train to Canterbury to register the death. Armed with the death certificate, I would now be able to set about notifying the various bodies of the passing of David. Meanwhile, I received more emails from Roy. One of them read:

"I called in to visit Ansley last evening (Sunday): 'David's brother Rick came to see me' She was delighted to meet you. She said that you were looking for a Will: Er – No Chance, two or three months back I called in on David one evening after he had been down to his local surgery: David told me that the nurse had taken him aside and sat down for a talk. Although he had been told some weeks before that the Doctor thought he only had six-twelve months to live, He was very upset and offended when the nurse said, 'Have you made a will?' Not an unreasonable question for a man of 71 in any case, but it would mean facing the grim reality. Then the nurse went on, "Well What About DNR – DO NOT RESUSCITATE, Do you want to be resuscitated? David was in tears putting both hands over his face just whilst telling me about it, saying, '*I Thought To My Self – Oh My God, Where Are We Going Now*!'. When David watched 'Children in Need' on T.V. - he had to change channels because they visited a Children's Hospice."

Roy was clearly not very fond of Ian, but I made it clear that I did not intend to get the police involved with the theft of David's things. I had also explained to both Ian and Roy that there would not be a funeral service but that the ashes would be scattered in Eastnor Park so that David could be reunited with his mother. I was hoping that this would be the last time that I had to deal with either Ian or Roy. I had learned much from them about David's life and character. He led quite a sad life really and died with very few friends. I was just pleased that I had found him four years earlier, otherwise he may have died with none of the family knowing.

David was cremated on 23rd December 2019, at the Garden of England Crematorium in Sittingbourne, Kent. In the first week of the new year, I once again boarded the train for Kent. On arrival in Sittingbourne, I hopped on the bus to the crematorium and collected David. It did feel rather strange packing the container, which held his ashes, into my backpack. It was the first time I had given David a piggyback ride. Maybe, a repayment for those childhood days at Eastnor when we used to jump on his back when we play wrestled with him. I visited a heritage shop in Sittingbourne where I was able to purchase a booklet about Cryalls House. It was the same booklet that had been given to me when I last visited the house ten years earlier. I had given my original copy to Bob. I had already decided that David and I would visit the house again that afternoon, so I set off to walk down Borden Lane. The long, straight drive from the main road had long gone, having been built on, but the house had not changed much since the last visit. I rang the doorbell and was greeted by a new owner. He was most welcoming and offered to show me round the garden and was keen to chat about my experience of living there over fifty years previously. I explained that, since I was so young at the time, that I did not remember very much. I did say that my earliest memory was of standing on the circular patch of grass in front of the house and seeing an aeroplane fly overhead. The owner said he had an aerial picture of Cryalls House from a time before the orchards surrounding the property had been replaced by a housing estate. He fetched the photo and I studied it with interest. It was, indeed, pretty much how I had remembered the house and garden from the 1960s. I was, however, slightly disappointed that there was not a little boy on the lawn, staring up at the aircraft that took the photo!

I messaged both Peta and Colin to confirm that I had collected David's remains and that we were paying a visit to our old house. Peta wished she had been able to visit too, just for the memories. She mentioned the time that she had been attacked. I had forgotten all about that incident and asked her for more detail. Peta had been set upon by a man, in Borden Lane, and was knocked to the ground. Fortunately, David and Bob were nearby and were able to chase the assailant away and he ran off down the lane. Peta would have been about eleven years old then with David fourteen and Bob thirteen years old. Although it sounded like a rather nasty incident, it was the first time that I had really thought about my three oldest siblings being children. Just as I had been close to Simon and Colin when we used to play as children, I realised that David, Bob and Peta would have had similar experiences together.

It was quite appropriate that I took David's ashes to Cryalls House. It was where we were living when Dad was posted in Cyprus. He did not take the family with him, and it was whilst in Cyprus that he met Claire. His time with Mum was over for good. Yet it was probably getting Mum pregnant with David in 1947 that had led to Mum taking the identity of Marie Cremin and starting the mystery that I had been trying to solve. David had returned to the place where we were last a complete family. Now, both my parents were dead, as were three of my brothers, and I was still no nearer to finding out who Mum was. All I knew was that, at this house, once lived five brothers and their sister, along with Arthur and Helen.

11. AUDREY

The trip to Sittingbourne in January 2020 seemed like a good place to end my story about the family. It was the place where we had all been together as a family for the last time and it looked like I was never going to solve the mystery of Mum's real identity. Tim had continued to look at the DNA results without success and Peta had not submitted her sample, so we were unlikely to get further DNA matches to investigate. Then, in March, the world was struck with the coronavirus crisis and normal life was put on hold. It would be months before I would be able to travel to various places again. At least with the internet, I would be able to do some searching online. One positive outcome of Covid-19 was the discovery of Zoom. Through Zoom meetings, I was able to chat more frequently with Tim, and the rest of the family, more than ever before. Even though we were kept apart by Covid, it brought us together! Despite that, it still seemed extremely unlikely that we would make any significant progress in our quest for the truth about Mum.

In the end, the Covid-19 pandemic meant that travel

ground to a halt for well over a year. I was not able to fly to Malta to visit Claire. We did book a flight to travel to Malta, but another outbreak of the virus meant that we were unable to go. We kept in contact with Claire by phoning her three times a week. The staff at her care home were also in lockdown. They had to live at the home and were not able to leave the building. No visitors were allowed, so Claire's only contact with the outside world was by telephone and letters. Unfortunately, during the year, her health deteriorated, and she was admitted to Mater Dei hospital in Malta. At least Claire was now able to be visited by Andre, Guido (an old friend and helper) and the priest from Claire's church. On 28th February 2021, Claire passed away peacefully. It was just three days after the funeral of her old friend, Catherine, whom we had visited in Pembrokeshire. We had lost two wonderful women who had brought sunshine into our lives. I had known both less than three years, but they would be greatly missed, particularly Claire. She had been the link back to the father that I never really knew.

A new television series began on BBC, '*DNA, Family Secrets*', which looked at how DNA tests could help trace family members and help in looking for hereditary conditions. I wish I had known when they were producing the programme and submitted my problem. Maybe they could have done Tim's task for him but having greater access to resources to help trace Mum. I decided to look up other sites that did DNA tests. I had, on Tim's recommendation, used Ancestry UK. Would I get different matches if I used another provider? I decided to apply for a DNA test with MyHeritage and ordered a test kit. The DNA test kits were at a discounted price but it was still an expensive gamble.

Whilst on the MyHeritage site, I searched for my father, Arthur Walter Lovering. Several results appeared including two which referred to two of his siblings, so was clearly the same Arthur. I could not see the details of the results of the search unless I paid a subscription. I did not intend to join another group but I was getting desperate to make some progress. I stumped up more money for a year's subscription to MyHeritage. I then noticed that the results had Arthur dying in 1946. For a moment, I was taken aback. Did the real Arthur die in 1946 and my father assumed his identity? It would be at about the same time that Mum became Marie Cremin. Were both of my parents identity thieves? I then realised that the person submitting those results must have mistaken Arthur's father, Leonard's date of death for his. Leonard died in 1946. So, no identity theft, but it would have made a rather astonishing twist to my family story.

Some of my friends asked whether the book was finished. I told them that it was effectively completed, but I still had no ending. The mystery was still a mystery.

"Well, why don't you just make up an ending then?"

I did not feel comfortable with that suggestion although, all along, we had come up with theories about Mum's background and where she came from. We had accrued very little evidence about her, although we had established that she was not Marie Cremin. All we had were the various stories she had told us about her early life but which of them, if any, were true?

Supposing, apart from the Marie Cremin bits, everything that she had described over the years was actually true, what would that suggest about her life? Here is my version, based on her 'facts':

Helen Truthful was born in North London, to very middle-class parents, on 12th May 1923. I am saying 1923 as that would have made her ten years older than Dad, something I remember her telling me when I was young. Her father was a diplomat, or similar, which meant that he travelled to various places around the world whilst Helen was growing up. He was a keen Arsenal fan and would tell Helen stories about the great Herbert Chapman team and its star striker, Ted Drake. Her father had always been a superb sportsman and had represented Cambridge University in the annual Varsity rugby match versus Oxford at Twickenham. Helen's father was posted in New Zealand for a year and, during this time, Helen remembered a trip to Lake Taupo on North Island. These were some of her earliest memories and the Maori people rubbing their noses together to greet each other made a huge impression on her. Later, her father's work took him back to Europe and the family spent several years in Germany. It was the mid-1930s and Hitler and the Nazi Party were on the rise. The family went along to one of the Nuremburg Rallies and were mesmerised by the adulation that Hitler got from the crowd. The family also lived for a few months in Moscow and Helen's best friend was a young Russian girl. To communicate with her, Helen picked up the rudiments of the Russian language.

On the family's return to Germany, her parents decided that it would be best if Helen attended a Convent school in Louvain, over the border in Belgium. Helen did not enjoy the strictness of the nuns' teachings at the school and only remembers her days there spent kneeling on the cold stone slabs of the chapel, having to chant her 'Hail Marys' as part of a punishment. As the threat of war hung over Europe, the family returned to England and back to London. Helen did well academically and found herself a place at Bedford College in London, studying History. She lived at home with her parents which was quite close to a German POW camp. Near to Christmas time, she could hear the German prisoners singing 'Silent night'. For the rest of her life, whenever she heard the carol, it would take her back to those wartime years in London. Helen was determined to play her part in the war effort, but she was still a minor, being under twenty-one years old. She decided that she would lie about her age so that she could join the Women's Auxiliary Air Force. She was posted to Fighter Command HQ, not far away from where she lived. Helen would be one of the women in the control room that plotted the positions of squadrons on the table map. After the war, she returned to her studies and got a job in a bar to help pay the bills. It was whilst working in a bar one night, that she met Arthur, a handsome army officer, who had recently returned from serving in the Far East. He told Helen the story of how he had returned from fighting in Italy during the War only to find his wife had got pregnant with another man. One thing led to another and, a couple of months later, Helen discovered that she was pregnant. Arthur was rather horrified as, technically, he was still married and, being an officer, getting his mistress pregnant was not socially acceptable. Helen wanted to keep the child so they both agreed that Helen should pretend to be Arthur's wife. Helen was now Marie, though her friends would still call her Helen. She had to pretend that her parents had gone on holiday to Cork in Ireland where her mother gave birth to her. Helen began the lie that she lived with for the rest of her life.

Alternatively, Mum made up all the stories about Belgium, New Zealand, Bedford College, joining the WAAFs and so on. What was the true story in that case?

Hilda Bullshit was born in 1925. Her parents were both hard-working and ensured that Hilda had a good upbringing. She was well educated and did well at school. Hilda wanted to go to university, but her parents could not afford for her to continue her studies beyond school. She helped in her parents' business during the war. Her father was called up to the army, despite his advancing years, and Hilda had to get other work to help the family survive. She got a job working behind the bar in a local pub where she often chatted with service personnel from the nearby Fighter Command HQ. One of her best friends worked in the control room and would tell Hilda of the devastating times when they heard that some pilots had been shot down during an operation. She would describe how a place at the dining table was left empty, to show where the missing pilot would have sat. One evening, after the war had finished, a handsome soldier entered the pub and got chatting with Hilda. He was full of interesting tales of his times fighting in Italy, including at the siege of Monte Cassino, and about how, on his return, he found his home had been bombed. He then discovered his wife, in another man's home, with a young baby in her arms. He told her that he had immediately signed up with the army again and asked to be posted as far away as possible. His heart was broken and he felt that he could never love a woman again. He confessed that Hilda was the first woman he had met who really cared about him. Hilda and Arthur began an affair and Hilda got pregnant with David.

The truth was probably a mixture of these two stories.

There were still Covid-19 restrictions and large numbers of infections with the omicron variant as we entered 2022. It was Tim's birthday in January, so I sent him good wishes and also mentioned that the 1921 National Census had been made available to the public. The Census was taken every ten years to collect data on the population which could, amongst other things, be used to guide policy making. The data is only made available to the general public after one hundred years. I did not think there would be much for us to find on the 1921 Census. The 1931 Census would be of more interest but the records for England and Wales had been destroyed in a fire during the Second World War. Tim thanked me and teased me by saying that he had made some progress on the DNA research but needed to explain it verbally, rather than by email. I was intrigued, but it would have to wait as we were both busy that day. Meanwhile, Tim sent me an extract from the 1921 Census including my grandfather, Leonard Brasier Lovering. He was living with his second wife, Ethel, in 1921, along with their daughter, Violet, and Ethel's daughter from a previous relationship, Dora. Later Tim sent me the entry which included my father, Arthur, with his mother and three brothers. My father had not appeared in the 1911 Census so, consequently, many Lovering family trees on the genealogical sites omitted him.

Two days later, I spoke to Tim via Zoom. Colin also joined us from Romania to hear what Tim had discovered. Tim delighted in informing us that he was quite confident that he had narrowed down which family that Mum might have come from. He had been helped by information given by my DNA results on the MyHeritage genealogical site. I felt really pleased as I had gambled on paying a hefty fee to get a DNA test on a different site in the hope that it would yield some alternative matches to Ancestry UK. The key match was someone called Martin Russell. He was marked as a possible second cousin, a close match to me. Tim has used Martin Russell, and his relatives, to triangulate with other people in his research. That had led him to find possible grandparents of Mum! Tim felt there was a strong chance that his deductions were correct.

Colin and I were on tenterhooks. Who were Mum's grandparents? Tim then announced that her grandfather was probably a John Church who was married to Emily Filer. The amazing thing was that Tim told us that they came from Paulton and Clutton, towns in Somerset, not that far away from us in Bristol! Martin Russell's parents were Douglas Russell and June Church. His mother was related to John Church, hence the strong DNA match. One of John and Emily's children was called Mabel. Mabel had married John Stone but appeared to have moved to

London in 1921. Tim had strong suspicions that Mabel might be Mum's mother. Could we, at last, be close to solving the mystery of Mum's identity? We still needed to do further research to find out but, after all these years, we had something tangible to investigate. I was a little surprised to learn that Mum's family might be from the south-west of England. By moving to Bristol in 1985, had I returned to my family roots? A girl called Samantha Church had been one of my pupils at Brimsham Green School in the 1990s. Maybe she a relative. Strangely, I knew Samantha's Mum as she worked in the local Fishponds branch of Barclay's Bank. Church was quite a common name in the area so there was probably no connection, but who knows?

After the Zoom call ended, I did a little research of my own. I messaged Martin Russell to see if we could find out more about the Church family. On Ancestry, I found another family tree that included Mabel Church. Documents attached to the tree told me that she lived in Hornsey, north London. That would fit in with Mum's tales of going to watch Arsenal football team play. Arsenal's old ground, Highbury Stadium, is in that part of London. I sent an email to Tim with my thoughts about Mabel moving to Hornsey.

He replied: "Interesting. If we assume she (Mum) was registered as 'Church', with mother's name 'Church' and look only in the locale of Arsenal (Hackney and Central London) and restrict to 1920-1930, we only have six people remaining. If we further assume her birthday was really in May, we have only two people left: Kathleen A

Church and Constance Church. Constance seems a bit late, but Kathleen might be worth a look"

I continued my research and found a family tree, that had been produced by another person. That tree included Mabel Church and her children. I posted another email to Tim!

I wrote: "This family tree shows Mabel having three children. The order suggests that the eldest was Frederick, born 1920. Does that mean that Mabel left her husband and headed to London to start a new life and, in May 1925, gave birth to a daughter, Kathleen? Had she already reverted to her maiden name?"

Tim answered promptly: "I don't think she was married when Frederick was born. He was living with her parents in 1921, while she was an unmarried servant in Bristol, so I guess she got pregnant, went home to have the baby, then went back to work"

Me: "Do you know anything about the other two children in that family tree?"

Tim: "No, I don't- they could be someone's guess, of course. There are a bunch of births in Clutton around that time that look illegitimate (mothers' surname Church) but, actually, they are a product of a marriage between two Churches"

As I mentioned earlier, Church was a common name in that part of the country. The 'someone's guess' that Tim referred to was something that I had done when putting together my family tree. It was not always obvious how people were related so they were added, even though it was not always certain to be correct.

Another thing I found on the new family tree I had discovered was a photo of a woman who, if Tim's suggestions were correct, would have been Mum's cousin. The photo was not of great quality, but there were definitely similarities between her and Mum… or were there? Maybe I was looking for something that was not there just to raise my hopes that we were close to solving the puzzle. I was partly re-assured when Colin agreed with me about her likeness to Mum.

I carried out further investigations into the Church family in Somerset. Mum's possible grandparents, John and Emily Church, were buried in Paulton Cemetery. I looked at the website for the cemetery and was pleasantly surprised to find that there was a map of the cemetery with each burial plot labelled. If only all cemeteries did that. It could have saved me many hours of wandering amongst gravestones in the past. I quickly found the plot where John and Emily were buried. The cemetery itself was just a short drive from my son, Michael's, new home near Radstock. I sent a message to Michael to inform him of Tim's news and that his great-great-grandparents might be buried near him. Michael visited the cemetery a day or two later and found their burial plot. Sadly, there was no headstone.

Tim had given me two possible people who might be Mum, Kathleen and Constance. Of the two, Tim felt that Kathleen was more likely due to her year of birth matching that of what we thought was Mum's. I had joked that Kathleen was a good Irish name though, of course, we were now quite certain that Mum had no connection with Ireland. Where did the name Helen come from? Maybe, Mum was adopted and her new parents gave her a different name. I noticed that the last five letters of Kathleen was an anagram of Helen. It could be that Mum made up a new name for herself. It would not be the last time that she did that! I decided that I needed to order a copy of Kathleen's birth certificate to help confirm our suspicions or, probably more likely, to tell us that Kathleen was not Mum. The certificate would give us details of her parents. Was Mabel her mother? It would also reveal Kathleen's date of birth. If that was 12th May, the day that Mum celebrated her birthday, it would be difficult to deny that Mum was really Kathleen. I duly ordered the birth certificate using an online service. I would now have to wait for a copy of the birth certificate. It would be a nervous wait that would not be helped by the effect the Omicron variant of Covid was having on the population. People were having to isolate if they tested positive for coronavirus. There had been many staff absentees and several public businesses were struggling to maintain a normal service. We had gone three days without receiving any mail. It could be a longer wait that we would like before the birth certificate arrived.

As it turned out, I only had to wait nine days. I came back from a long walk to find the post had been delivered. Amongst the pile of mail was a brown envelope and, on the back, it indicated that it was from the General Register Office. I excitedly went in the front room to tell Pauline that the certificate had arrived. I opened the letter and took out the birth certificate. The first thing that I noticed was the registration date: 'twenty-second June 1925'. I thought that this was quite late if Kathleen was born on same day as Mum's birthday. I then scanned across to the 'When and where born' section: 'twelfth May 1925 Mothers Hospital'. For a moment, I was in a spin and had to think when Mum's birthday was. Yes, it was 12th May, the same as Kathleen's!

"It must be her! Kathleen must be Mum!". I was very excited. I read more of the birth certificate. Her name was given as 'Kathleen Audrey'. Audrey! On Peta's birth certificate, Mum had put her name down as Marie Hilda Audrey. It could not be a coincidence that Kathleen was called Audrey too. I took this as further confirmation that we had found Mum.

I felt exhilarated that it our long search was over and I had to tell everyone. It brought to mind the scene in the film '*The Killing Fields*' where the journalist, Sydney Schanberg, hears the news that Dith Pran had been found. Schanberg had left Pran to the mercy of the Khmer Rouge regime in Cambodia and felt immense guilt as there was no contact with Pran for several years. Schanberg runs round the newsroom telling everyone that Pran had been found and phones his family. I had to do the same. I sent a copy of the birth certificate to Tim and Colin stating that we had found her! I then forwarded copies to other members of the family. Tim commented that he was amazed how it had all come together. I felt joy that after all this time, we had finally found what we were looking for.

I studied the other details on the birth certificate. As expected, there was a blank space where the name of the father should be. Maybe, Tim might want to embark on another DNA search to find possible candidates for Mum's biological father. He would have to eliminate all the DNA matches associated with both my Dad and Kathleen Church first. The certificate stated that Kathleen's mum was Mabel Jessie Church. That also confirmed that we had the birth certificate for Mum as it was through Tim's DNA research that Mabel had been identified as a possible mother of Mum. Mabel was a Domestic Servant at 'Hillcote', Lyndhurst Gardens in Hampstead. Kathleen (Mum) had been born in the Mothers Hospital. I looked this up on the internet and discovered it was in Hackney and ran by The Salvation Army.

On the extreme right of the birth certificate was, not unexpectedly, a note to say that Kathleen had subsequently been adopted. It had appeared that Mabel had left her husband in Somerset and moved to London alone, not that we knew this for sure. Given no father was named, Kathleen was probably an unplanned child and Mabel was probably in no position to raise her alone. I wondered whether her boss at 'Hillcote' might know something about it! Whatever, the situation, Mabel had Kathleen adopted. Kathleen's adoption parents might well have changed her name, maybe to Hilda Audrey or Helen Audrey. I would have to carry out further research to find out Kathleen's new surname. I had often referred to the list of Cambridge rugby Blues during our long search. It could still be that Mum's father, her adopted father, appears on that list. There could be difficulty researching adoption records, particularly as we had no exact proof that Kathleen was really our mother. Tim suspected that Data Protection laws may mean we would have to wait until a hundred years after the birth (in 2025) until we could find the information. I contacted a 'Family Finder' company on the internet. I spoke to a man and told him about our search for Mum and what we wanted to know. I also mentioned Tim's concern and the man said that he thought it would not be a problem. I was very encouraged by that, until he then outlined the costs. He quoted a figure of £1660 early on and I stopped him. I informed him that the price was rather higher than expected. We could not afford that, much as it would be great to know Mum's adopted name. Who knows, her adopted parents might well have been diplomats or explorers and travelled to New Zealand, Russia and Germany. It could be that Mum was Helen Truthful after all.

I had emailed several more family researchers, as well as The Salvation Army, regarding accessing adoption records and, a few days later, another responded. I gave her my details and she phoned me soon after. The woman was most helpful as she gave me some advice before we even got round to discussing any business. When I told her about Mum using Marie's name on our birth certificates, she said it was not illegal to use another name. That surprised me. She then asked whether I had access to the 1939 Census and, if so, suggested searching for Kathleen Audrey, but keep surname blank. She explained that many adoption families kept the first names, particularly those that were less wealthy. I told her that I suspected that my nephew, Tim, would have already done that and, also that we had our suspicions that Mum was adopted into a well-to-do household (if her stories of travel around the world and going to university were true). The woman on the phone also asked if Mum had a passport as she had used the Passport Office in the past for her research. Mum and the family had travelled to and from Germany so she would have needed a passport. Did she hold a passport in her real name or Marie Lovering? Health records could also be a source of information, but access would be a problem. The researcher told me that she could take on my request at half the price of the other company I had contacted. She did, however, warn me that there could be several difficulties which could escalate the cost or lead to failure of the task. For example, Mum may have had siblings in her adopted family who may still be living. They would need to be contacted before any information could be released to me. I thanked the woman for her help. Tim later told me that the 1939 Census is redacted so that anyone still living would not be able to be identified. Since there would be no record of Kathleen's death, as Kathleen took the name Marie, she would not appear in the records.

Not long after, I got a response from The Salvation Army. It was an email from Major Kevin Pooley, Social Historian from the International Heritage Centre. He wrote:

"Please find attached transcripts of interview notes for Mabel, as well as discharge records for her and Kathleen.

Unfortunately, there is no mention of the adoption agency involved - this was apparently organised after Kathleen left the home. I have also included some material that I mention in the transcripts for background."

I opened the attachment which was labelled 'Lovering'. It contained a transcript of notes taken soon after the birth of Kathleen. It read:

"Extracted from Women's Social Work Applicants' Secretary's Interview Book 79 (General) March 1925 to June 1926, page 114

Miss Mabel Church
Self
age 28
Maternity. Brought by nurse from situation. Was taken home to Bristol yesterday but brothers refused to stay if mother kept her. She returned to London this morning. We would receive girl early next week if mistress could keep till then. Spoke with her on telephone. Very kind. Cannot have girl – but will pay for lodgings until we can receive her. Said we would arrange this. Mistress – Mrs Horne. 'Hilcote'. Lyndhurst. Gardens. Hampstead. Parents – Mr & Mrs Church. Church Street. Paulton. Bristol. Girl has £10:0:0 Mrs Horne will help with clothes. Cannot say who will take child. Is insured & payments are to date. Man responsible, Robert Macdonald (Chef) 33 Belsize Sq. N.W.1. but has since left here & no address. Said he would stand by her. Willing he should pay. Willing to stay. Mother has her insured. Thinks parents will arrange about baby in case of death. Sent to '259'. medical satisfactory. April 17th Wrote Mrs Horne giving girl's address as 'Cotland' & mentioning baby clothes. April 21st Mrs Horne sends £3.3.0 We thank Mrs Horne & arrange with '259' for

girl to go tomorrow to 'Cotland'.

They wish us to find foster mother. "   (Note: '259'
refers to the address of the home)

The notes were not easy to follow but they confirmed
that we had the correct Mabel Church found through the
DNA matches. She had taken Kathleen back to her
family in Bristol. It appeared that the new born baby was
not welcomed by her brothers. Then I noticed the key
piece of information. The man responsible was Robert
Macdonald. I assumed that meant that he was Kathleen's
father and that was confirmed in the details that
followed. Robert was Mum's father, my grandfather! He
was a chef and, probably, a Scotsman. I most likely had
two grandparents from a Scottish background: Dad's
mother and Mum's father. I read the notes again and
realised that Robert had said that he would stand by her
but had left the address that he had given. It appeared
that he had not stayed to support his daughter after all.
Very sad. That would have explained why Mabel had
asked to find a foster mother and that Kathleen was later
adopted.

I forwarded the email to Tim who was pleased, and
astonished, by the rapid response from The Salvation
Army and the information it had provided. We now had
the identity of Mum's father so Tim would not have to
carry out another DNA search to find him. His next task
would be to find who Robert was and whether he linked
into the DNA trees that Tim had put together. After a
day or two, Tim informed me that he had found a

probable match for Robert Macdonald. He was Robert Johnstone Macdonald and was born in Caithness, Scotland. There was an added complication as it appeared that both he and his mother were illegitimate. A theme of illegitimate children in Mum's family was emerging. It was not that surprising given that me and my siblings were also born out of wedlock!

Karen, Simon's widow, had been sorting through some of Simon's stuff. It was over five years since we had lost him and, only now, did Karen feel she could look at Simon's things. She sent me some old photos and documents. Amongst them was a letter from Tim, sent in 2008, that outlined some facts about our ancestors along the male line. It was good to see the births, deaths, occupations, spouses, etc presented concisely, but there was some information missing. It made me appreciate how much family research we had done since then and the things we had uncovered. For example, the sorry tale of my uncle, Sidney, who had lived his final years in a mental hospital. With Simon's papers was a record of Tim's emails with Sidney's son, Barry, who living in Florida. I had similar email communications with Barry a few years afterwards. I had lost contact with him again and wondered if he was still alive.

It was now nearly forty years since I had heard Simon tell me that Mum had said, "Your father and I never married". That phrase had started my long search into finding Mum's real name and, along the way, I had found out a great deal about my family and other Loverings around the world. After all that time, I now had an answer.

Mum had been born Kathleen Audrey Church and, after that, had been variously called, maybe, Helen, Hilda Audrey, Marie Lovering, Marie Barnes and whatever her adopted name was. I guess the most important name she had was Mum. It was only by writing this account that I really appreciated what a remarkable person she had been. It cannot have been easy to raise six children almost single-handedly and had to live with the lie of pretending to be someone else. Whatever her real name, she was my Mum.

My search had finished with the arrival of the copy of Mum's birth certificate. I had been trying to discover my mother's real name. I had regretted never asking Mum directly about it. The irony is that, because she was adopted, Mum probably did not know her real name either!

ABOUT THE AUTHOR

Rick Lovering is a retired secondary school teacher. He lives in Bristol with his wife, Pauline and has two grown-up children. He spent 38 years teaching mathematics. He is a life-long supporter of York City.

This is his first book.

Printed in Great Britain
by Amazon

80653001R00161